American Social History Since 1860

GOLDENTREE BIBLIOGRAPHIES
IN AMERICAN HISTORY
under the series editorship of
Arthur S. Link

American Social History Since 1860

compiled by

Robert H. Bremner

The Ohio State University

with the assistance of

Richard M. Friedman

and

Donald B. Schewe

The Ohio State University

AHM Publishing Corporation
Northbrook, Illinois 60062

Copyright © 1971
AHM PUBLISHING CORPORATION
All rights reserved

This book, or parts thereof, must not be used or reproduced in any manner without written permission. For information address the publisher, AHM PUBLISHING CORPORATION, 1500 Skokie Boulevard, Northbrook, Illinois 60062.

ISBN: Cloth — 0-88295-504-7
(Formerly 390-12112-6)
Paper — 0-88295-503-9
(Formerly 390-12111-8)

Library Of Congress Card Number: 70-146848

PRINTED IN THE UNITED STATES OF AMERICA
783
Second Printing

Editor's Foreword

GOLDENTREE BIBLIOGRAPHIES IN AMERICAN HISTORY are designed to provide students, teachers, and librarians with ready and reliable guides to the literature of American History in all its remarkable scope and variety. Volumes in the series cover comprehensively the major periods in American history, while additional volumes are devoted to all important subjects.

Goldentree Bibliographies attempt to steer a middle course between the brief list of references provided in the average textbook and the long bibliography in which significant items are often lost in the sheer number of titles listed. Each bibliography is, therefore, selective, with the sole criterion for choice being the significance—and not the age—of any particular work. The result is bibliographies of all works, including journal articles and doctoral dissertations, that are still useful, without bias in favor of any particular historiographical school.

Each compiler is a scholar long associated, both in research and teaching, with the period or subject of his volume. All compilers have not only striven to accomplish the objective of this series but have also cheerfully adhered to a general style and format. However, each compiler has been free to define his field, make his own selections, and work out internal organization as the unique demands of his period or subject have seemed to dictate.

The single great objective of *Goldentree Bibliographies in American History* will have been achieved if these volumes help researchers and students to find their way to the significant literature of American history.

                                                                Arthur S. Link

Preface

SOCIAL HISTORY IS the most permissive and loosely-defined area of historical study. The late Arthur M. Schlesinger, writing in 1937, half-seriously defined social history as a subject taught by persons who called themselves social historians. Thirty years later, Peter N. Stearns declared in the first issue of *The Journal of Social History*: "A certain degree of consensus exists, however fuzzy and inarticulate, among most social historians about what they are doing and why, and this is satisfactory for most purposes." But what do social historians teach? And what is their consensus? These are questions we have kept in mind and tried to answer in compiling the bibliography.

The selection and organization of entries indicate our sense of the present dimensions of American social history. As we see it, social history is not a precisely delimited field of study, but a way of looking at the past which seeks to recognize and reveal relationships among different aspects of human experience. Social history today, in addition to its traditional emphasis on everyday events and the life of the common man, pays increasing attention to the structure of society, social change and mobility, and styles of life in various classes and cultures. Because social history derives its data from a variety of sources, our list of books and articles necessarily draws upon other branches of history and many related disciplines.

Users of the bibliography may note the absence of titles which should have been listed and the inclusion of others which might be eliminated. We shall be grateful for suggestions, whether of additions or deletions, which will make periodic revision of the bibliography useful to students and teachers of American social history. This bibliography was selected from works published prior to June 30, 1970.

R. H. B.

R. M. F.

D. B. S.

Abbreviations

Ag Hist	Agricultural History
Atl Monthly	Atlantic Monthly
Am Hist Rev	American Historical Review
Am Jew Archiv	American Jewish Archives
Am J Public Health	American Journal of Public Health
Am Q	American Quarterly
Am W	American West
Ann Am Acad Pol Soc Sci	Annals, American Academy of Political and Social Science
Antioch Rev	Antioch Review
Bull Hist Philos Soc Ohio	Bulletin of the Historical and Philosophical Society of Ohio
Bull Hist Med	Bulletin of the History of Medicine
Bus Hist Rev	Business History Review
Cal Hist Soc Q	California Historical Society Quarterly
Church Hist	Church History
Chris Cent	Christian Century
Civil War Hist	Civil War History
Cur Hist	Current History
Explor Entrep Hist	Explorations in Entrepreneurial History
Fla Hist Q	Florida Historical Quarterly
Harv Ed Rev	Harvard Educational Review
Hist Ed Q	History of Education Quarterly
Hunt Lib Q	Huntington Library Quarterly
Ind Mag Hist	Indiana Magazine of History
J Amer Hist	Journal of American History
J Econ Hist	Journal of Economic History
J Inter-Am Stud	Journal of Inter-American Studies
J Miss Hist	Journal of Mississippi History
J Neg Educ	Journal of Negro Education
J Neg Hist	Journal of Negro History
J Pol Econ	Journal of Political Economy
J S Hist	Journal of Southern History
J Soc Hist	Journal of Social History
J Hist Ideas	Journal of the History of Ideas
Jour Q	Journalism Quarterly
Lab Hist	Labor History
La Hist	Louisiana History
Mich Hist	Michigan History
Mid-Am	Mid-America
Mil Affairs	Military Affairs
Minn Hist	Minnesota History
Miss Val Hist Rev	Mississippi Valley Historical Review
Mo Lab Rev	Monthly Labor Review

ABBREVIATIONS

Pac Hist Rev	Pacific Historical Review
Pol Sci Q	Political Science Quarterly
Proc Am Philos Soc	Proceedings, American Philosophical Society
Soc Casework	Social Casework
Soc Res	Social Research
Soc Svc Rev	Social Service Review
S Atl Q	South Atlantic Quarterly
SW Soc Sc Q	Southwestern Social Science Quarterly
Stetson Univ Bull	Stetson University Bulletin
Stud Left	Studies on the Left
Va Q Rev	Virginia Quarterly Review
W Pa Hist Mag	Western Pennsylvania Historical Magazine

NOTE: *Items marked by a (†) are available in paperback edition at the time this bibliography goes to press. The publisher and compiler invite suggestions for additions to future editions of the bibliography.*

Contents

Editor's Foreword   v

Preface   vii

Abbreviations   ix

I. Bibliographical Guides, Selected Reference and Historiographical Works   1

II. General Surveys of American Social History and American Society
   A. *General*   3
   B. *The Civil War and Reconstruction*   4
   C. *Late Nineteenth Century America*   5
   D. *The Progressive Era and World War I*   6
   E. *Between the Two Wars*   7
   F. *World War II and the Aftermath*   9
   G. *The 1950's and 1960's*   9

III. The Nation and Its Sections
   A. *General*   10
   B. *New England* (Me., N.H., Vt., Mass., R.I., Conn.)   10
   C. *The Middle Atlantic States* (N.Y., N.J., Pa.)   10
   D. *The North Central States* (Ohio, Ind., Ill., Mich., Wis.)   10
   E. *The Border States* (Del., Md., D.C., W.Va., Ky., Tenn.)   11
   F. *The Southern States* (Va., N.C., S.C., Ga., Fla., Ala., Miss., Ark., La.)   12
   G. *The West*   13
      1. General   13
      2. The Great Plains States (Minn., Iowa, Mo., N.D., S.D., Kan., Neb., Okla., Tex.)   14

		3. The Mountain States (Mont., Idaho, Wyo., Colo., N. Mex., Ariz., Utah, Nev.)	16
		4. The Pacific States (Wash., Ore., Calif., Alaska, Hawaii)	16
IV.	The Rise of the City		17
V.	The American People		
	A.	*Population and General Works* (including contemporary social surveys)	20
	B.	*Social Classes and Social Mobility*	21
	C.	*Internal Migration*	22
	D.	*Immigration*	22
		1. General	22
		2. Scandinavia (Norway, Sweden, Denmark, Finland)	23
		3. United Kingdom (England, Scotland, Wales, Ireland)	24
		4. Western Europe (France, Germany, Netherlands, Switzerland)	24
		5. Southern Europe (Italy, Greece)	24
		6. Eastern-Central Europe (Poland, Hungary, Yugoslavia)	25
		7. The Orient (China, Japan)	25
		8. The Americas	26
	E.	*Negroes*	26
		1. General	26
		2. Negro History	28
		3. Race Relations and Racial Protest	30
		4. Culture, Education, and Religion	31
		5. Employment	32
		6. Leadership	32
	F.	*Indians*	33
	G.	*Women*	34
	H.	*The Family*	36
	J.	*Children and Youth*	37
VI.	The American and His Work		
	A.	*General*	38
	B.	*Technology*	39
	C.	*Agriculture*	40

CONTENTS xiii

	1. General	40
	2. Rural Life	41
	3. Agrarian Discontent, Agrarian Movements and Government Policy	41
	4. Ranching and the Cowboy	42
	D. *Business, Commerce, and Industry*	43
	E. *Mining, Transportation, and Lumbering*	44
	F. *Professions, Clerical, and Service*	46
	G. *Military*	47
	H. *Labor*	48
	1. General	48
	2. Labor Unions	50
	3. Strikes	53

VII. The American and His Attitude Toward Other Americans
    A. *American Character*   53
    B. *Public Opinion*   55
    C. *Law and Justice*   55
    D. *Civil Liberties*   56
    E. *Segregation and Desegregation* (See also V E 3)   56
    F. *Nativism, Anti-Semitism, and Anti-Intellectualism*   57

VIII. The American and His Religious Life
    A. *General*   58
    B. *The Social Gospel*   60
    C. *Protestants and Protestantism*   61
    D. *Catholics and Catholicism*   63
    E. *Jews and Judaism*   63

IX. Social and Political Thought
    A. *General*   65
    B. *Radicalism*   67
    C. *Socialism*   68
    D. *Communism*   68
    E. *Liberalism*   69
    F. *Conservatism*   70
    G. *Utopianism*   71

X. Social Problems and Reform Movements
    A. *General*   71
    B. *Poverty*   72
    C. *Public Welfare and Social Security*   73

	D. *Housing*	74
	E. *Delinquency and Correction* (See also V J)	74
	F. *Philanthropy and Social Work*	75
	G. *Prohibition*	76
	H. *Conservation*	77
XI.	Cultural Life in America	
	A. *General Cultural Life*	78
	B. *Art, Architecture, and Music*	79
	C. *Language, Literature, and Drama*	82
	D. *Popular Culture*	84
	E. *Folklore and Folk Culture*	85
	F. *Recreation and Sports*	85
XII.	Education and Intellectual Trends	
	A. *General*	86
	B. *Elementary and Secondary*	87
	C. *Higher Education*	88
	D. *Libraries, Museums, and Learned Societies*	91
	E. *Intellectual Trends*	92
XIII.	Communications	
	A. *General*	94
	B. *Magazines*	95
	C. *Newspapers*	96
	D. *Book Publishing*	97
	E. *Radio and Television*	97
XIV.	Science	
	A. *General*	97
	B. *Health and Medicine*	98
	C. *Physical Sciences*	101
	D. *Social and Behavioral Sciences*	101
NOTES		103
INDEX		109

BIBLIOGRAPHY, REFERENCE, AND HISTORIOGRAPHY **I**

I. Bibliographical Guides, Selected Reference and Historiographical Works

1   AARON, Daniel et al. *Essays on History and Literature.* Ed. by Robert H. Bremner, Columbus, Ohio, 1966.

2   ADAMS, James T., ed. *Dictionary of American History.* 7 vols. New York, 1940–1963.

3   ADAMS, Ramon F. *The Rampaging Herd: A Bibliography of Books and Pamphlets on Men and Events in the Cattle Industry.* Norman, Okla., 1954.

4   American Historical Association. *Guide to Historical Literature.* New York, 1961.

5   American Historical Association. *Index to the Writings on American History, 1902–1940.* Washington, D.C., 1956.

6   American Historical Association. *Writings on American History.* 46 vols. Washington, D.C., 1902–1964.

7   American Jewish Periodical Center. *Jewish Newspapers and Periodicals on Microfilm, Available at the American Jewish Periodical Center.* Cincinnati, Ohio, 1957.

8   BASSETT, T. D. Seymour. "Bibliography: Descriptive and Critical." Vol. II of *Socialism and American Life.* Ed. by Donald D. Egbert and Stow Persons. 2 vols. Princeton, 1952.

9   BEERS, Henry P., comp. *Bibliographies in American History: Guide to Materials for Research.* Rev. ed. New York, 1942.

10 BERKHOFER, Robert F., Jr. *A Behavioral Approach to Historical Analysis.* New York, 1969.

11 BLAKE, Nelson M. *Novelists' America, 1910–1940.* Syracuse, 1970.

12 BLISS, W. D. P., ed. *The New Encyclopedia of Social Reform.* Rev. ed. New York, 1908.

13 BURR, Nelson R. "A Critical Bibliography of Religion in America." Vol. III and IV of *Religion in American Life.* Ed. by James W. Smith and A. Leland Jamison. 4 vols. Princeton, 1961.

14 *Dissertation Abstracts: A Guide to Dissertations and Monographs Available in Microfilm.* Ann Arbor, 1938– date. (Early volumes were titled *Microfilm Abstracts.*)

15 ELLIS, John Tracy. *Documents of American Catholic History.* Vol. 2. New York, 1961.

16 *Essay and General Literature Index.* New York, 1934– date.

17 FILLER, Louis. *A Dictionary of American Social Reform.* Yellow Springs, Ohio, 1964.

18 GOHDES, Clarence. *Literature and Theater of the States and Regions of the U.S.A.: An Historical Bibliography.* Durham, N.C., 1967.

2 BIBLIOGRAPHY, REFERENCE, AND HISTORIOGRAPHY

1. HAMER, Philip M., ed. *A Guide to Archives and Manuscripts in the United States.* New Haven, 1961.
2. HANDLIN, Oscar et al. *Harvard Guide to American History.* Cambridge, Mass., 1963.
3. HART, James D. *The Oxford Companion to American Literature.* New York, 1965.
4. HIGHAM, John, ed. *Reconstruction of American History.* New York, 1962.†
5. HOWE, George F. et al., eds. *The American Historical Association's Guide to Historical Literature.* New York, 1961.
6. JOHNSON, Allen, and Dumas MALONE, eds. *Dictionary of American Biography.* 22 vols. New York, 1928–1958.
7. JOHNSON, Thomas H. *The Oxford Companion to American History.* New York, 1966.
8. JONES, Howard Mumford, and Richard M. LUDWIG. *Guide to American Literature and Its Backgrounds Since 1890.* Cambridge, Mass., 1964.†
9. KAPLAN, Louis et al., eds. *A Bibliography of American Autobiographies.* Madison, Wis., 1961.
10. KUEHL, Warren F. *Dissertations in History: An Index to History Dissertations in American Universities, 1873–1960.* Lexington, Ky., 1965.
11. LILLARD, Richard G. *American Life in Autobiography: A Descriptive Guide.* Stanford, 1956.
12. LINGELBACH, William E., ed. *Approaches to American Social History.* New York, 1937.
13. Mc COUBREY, John W., ed. *American Art, Seventeen Hundred to Nineteen Hundred: Sources and Documents.* Englewood Cliffs, N.J., 1965.† (Sources and Documents in the *History of Art Series.*)
14. MILLER, Elizabeth W., ed. *The Negro in America: A Bibliography.* Cambridge, Mass., 1966.†
15. MORRIS, Richard B., ed. *Encyclopedia of American History.* Rev. ed. New York, 1961.†
16. National Research Council et al. *Doctoral Dissertations Accepted By American Universities....* 22 vols. New York, 1933–1955.
17. *National Union Catalogue of Manuscript Collections.* 5 vols. to date, plus indexes. Ann Arbor, Hamden, Conn., and Washington, D.C., 1962– date.
18. NEUFELD, Maurice F. *A Bibliography of American Labor History.* Ithaca, N.Y., 1964.
19. NEVINS, Allan, and Bell Irvin WILEY. *Civil War Books: A Critical Bibliography.* 2 vols. Baton Rouge, 1967–1969.
20. *Nineteenth Century Readers' Guide to Periodical Literature, 1890–1899.* 2 vols. New York, 1944.
21. *Readers' Guide to Periodical Literature.* New York, 1901– date.
22. SCHLESINGER, Arthur M. "What American Social History Is." *Harv Ed Rev*, VII (Jan. 1937), 57–65.

1   SPILLER, Robert E. et al., eds. *Literary History of the United States.* Vol. III: "Bibliography." New York, 1948. See also the "Bibliographical Supplement." Ed. by Richard M. Ludwig. New York, 1959.

2   STROUD, Gene S., and Gilbert E. DONAHUE, comps. *Labor History in the United States: A General Bibliography.* Urbana, Ill., 1961.

3   U.S. Bureau of the Census. *The Statistical History of the United States from Colonial Times to the Present.* Stamford, Conn., 1965.

4   U.S. Library of Congress. *A Guide to the Study of the United States of America.* Washington, D.C., 1960.

5   WARE, Caroline F. *The Cultural Approach to History.* New York, 1940.

6   WRIGHT, Lyle H. *American Fiction, 1851–1875: A Contribution Toward A Bibliography.* San Marino, Calif., 1957.

II. General Surveys of American Social History and American Society

A. General

7   ALLEN, Frederick Lewis. *The Big Change.* New York, 1952.†

8   BEARD, Charles A. and Mary R. *The Rise of American Civilization.* 4 vols. New York, 1927–1942.

9   BLAKE, Nelson M. *A History of American Life and Thought.* New York, 1963.

10 BOORSTIN, Daniel J. *An American Primer.* 2 vols. Chicago, 1966.†

11 BRAEMAN, John, et al., eds. *Change and Continuity in Twentieth Century America.* Columbus, Ohio, 1964.

12 HANDLIN, Oscar and Mary. *The Dimensions of Liberty.* Cambridge, Mass., 1961.

13 HOFSTADTER, Richard. *The Age of Reform: From Bryan to F.D.R.* New York, 1955.†

14 HOPKINS, J. G. E., and Florett ROBINSON, eds. *Album of American History.* Vol. V, 1917–1953. New York, 1960.

15 LERNER, Max. *America as a Civilization: Life and Thought in the United States Today.* New York, 1957.

16 LINK, Arthur S., and William B. CATTON. *American Epoch: A History of the U.S. Since the 1890's.* 3d ed. New York, 1967.†

17 MORISON, Elting E., ed. *The American Style: Essays in Value and Performance, A Report on the Dedham Conference of May 23–27, 1957.* New York, 1957.

18 MORRIS, Lloyd R. *Postscript to Yesterday; America: The Last Fifty Years.* New York, 1947.

4   SOCIAL HISTORY AND SOCIETY

1. President's Research Committee. *Recent Social Trends.* 2 vols. New York, 1933.
2. ROGERS, Agnes, and Frederick Lewis ALLEN. *The American Procession: American Life since 1860 in Photographs.* New York, 1933.
3. WISH, Harvey. *Society and Thought in Modern America: A Social and Intellectual History of the American People From 1865.* New York, 1962.
4. WOODWARD, William E. *The Way Our People Lived: An Intimate American History.* New York, 1944.

B. The Civil War and Reconstruction

5. BENTLEY, George R. *A History of the Freedmen's Bureau.* Philadelphia, 1955.
6. BROWN, Dee. *The Year of the Century: 1876.* New York, 1966.
7. BRUCE, Robert V. *1877: Year of Violence.* Indianapolis, 1959.
8. BUCK, Paul H. *The Road to Reunion, 1865–1900.* Gloucester, Mass., 1959.†
9. BURN, James D. *Three Years Among the Working-Classes in the United States During the War.* London, 1865.
10. COULTER, E. Merton. *The South During Reconstruction, 1865–1877.* Baton Rouge, 1947.
11. EATON, Clement. *A History of the Southern Confederacy.* New York, 1954.†
12. FITE, David E. *Social and Industrial Conditions in the North During the Civil War.* New York, 1962.
13. FRANKLIN, John Hope. *Reconstruction: After the Civil War.* Chicago, 1961.†
14. GATES, Paul W. *Agriculture and the Civil War.* New York, 1965.
15. HIGGINSON, Thomas Wentworth. *Army Life in a Black Regiment.* East Lansing, Mich., 1960.†
16. MARTIN, Edgar W. *The Standard of Living in 1860.* Chicago, 1942.
17. MASSEY, Mary Elizabeth. *Bonnet Brigades.* New York, 1966.
18. MASSEY, Mary Elizabeth. *Refugee Life in the Confederacy.* Baton Rouge, 1964.
19. NEVINS, Allan. *The Emergence of Modern America, 1865–1878.* New York, 1927.
20. NEVINS, Allen. *The War for the Union.* 2 vols. to date. New York, 1959–1960.
21. RANDALL, James G., and David DONALD. *The Civil War and Reconstruction.* 2d ed. Boston, 1961.

1 REID, Whitelaw. *After the War: A Tour of the Southern States, 1865–1866.* Ed. by C. Vann Woodward. New York, 1965.†

2 REZNECK, Samuel. "Distress, Relief and Discontent During the Depression of 1873–78." *J Pol Econ*, LVIII (1950), 494–512.

3 SEABROOK, Isaac D. *Before and After, or The Relations of the Races at the South.* Ed. by John Hammond Moore. Baton Rouge, 1967.

4 SMITH, George W., and Charles JUDAH. *Life in the North During the Civil War: A Source History.* Albuquerque, N.M., 1966.

5 STAMPP, Kenneth M. *The Era of Reconstruction.* New York, 1965.†

6 TROWBRIDGE, John T. *The Desolate South, 1865–1866.* Ed. by Gordon Carroll. New York, 1956.

7 UNGAR, Irwin. *The Greenback Era: A Social and Political History of American Finance, 1865–1879.* Princeton, 1964.

8 WALKER, Peter F. *Vicksburg: A People at War, 1860–1865.* Chapel Hill, 1960.

9 WILEY, Bell Irvin. *The Plain People of the Confederacy.* Baton Rouge, 1944.

10 WINTERS, John D. *The Civil War in Louisiana.* Baton Rouge, 1963.

C. Late Nineteenth Century America

11 BEER, Thomas. *The Mauve Decade: American Life at the End of the Nineteenth Century.* New York, 1926.†

12 FAULKNER, Harold U. *Politics, Reform and Expansion, 1890–1900.* New York, 1958.†

13 FINE, Sidney. *Laissez Faire and the General Welfare State.* Ann Arbor, Mich., 1956.†

14 GARRATY, John A. *The New Commonwealth, 1877–1890.* New York, 1968.†

15 GINGER, Ray. *Altgeld's America: The Lincoln Ideal versus Changing Realities.* Chicago, 1958.†

16 GINGER, Ray. *Age of Excess: The United States from 1877 to 1914.* New York, 1965.†

17 HARRIS, Neil, ed. *The Land of Contrasts, 1880–1901.* New York, 1970.

18 HAYS, Samuel P. *The Response to Industrialism, 1885–1914.* Chicago, 1957.†

19 LEECH, Margaret. *In the Days of McKinley.* New York, 1959.

20 MANN, Arthur. *Yankee Reformers in the Urban Age.* New York, 1954.†

21 MORGAN, H. Wayne. *William McKinley and His America.* Syracuse, 1963.

1 MORGAN, H. Wayne, ed. *The Gilded Age: A Reappraisal.* Syracuse, 1970.
2 MUMFORD, Lewis. *The Brown Decades.* Gloucester, Mass., 1960.†
3 REZNECK, Samuel. "Unemployment, Unrest, and Relief in the United States during the Depression of 1893–1897." See 5.12.
4 SHANNON, Fred A. *The Centennial Years: A Political and Economic History of America from the Late 1870's to the Early 1890's.* Ed. by Robert Huhn Jones. Garden City, N.Y., 1967.†
5 STEEPLES, Douglas W. "The Panic of 1893. Contemporary Reflections and Reactions." *Mid-Am*, XLVII (1965), 155–175.
6 WEBB, Beatrice. *Beatrice Webb's American Diary, 1898.* Ed. by David A. Shannon. Madison, Wis., 1963.
7 WIEBE, Robert H. *The Search for Order, 1877–1920.* New York, 1967.†
8 WOODWARD, C. Vann. *Origins of the New South, 1887–1920.* Baton Rouge, 1951.†
9 ZIFF, Larzer. *The American Eighteen Nineties: Life and Times of a Lost Generation.* New York, 1966.†

D. The Progressive Era and World War I

10 ADDAMS, Jane. *Twenty Years at Hull House.* New York, 1910.†
11 CHURCHILL, Allen. *Over Here! An Informal Re-creation of the Home Front in World War I.* New York, 1968.
12 FAULKNER, Harold U. *The Decline of Laissez Faire, 1897–1917.* New York, 1951.†
13 FAULKNER, Harold U. *Politics, Reform, and Expansion: 1890–1900.* See 5.12.
14 FAULKNER, Harold U. *The Quest for Social Justice, 1898–1914.* New York, 1931.
15 FILLER, Louis. *Muckrakers: Crusaders for American Liberalism.* Chicago, 1968.
16 HARBAUGH, William H. *Power and Responsibility: The Life and Times of Theodore Roosevelt.* New York, 1961.
17 LEUCHTENBURG, William E. *The Perils of Prosperity, 1914–1932.* Chicago, 1958.†
18 LINK, Arthur S. *Woodrow Wilson and the Progressive Era, 1910–1917.* New York, 1954.†
19 LORD, Walter. *The Good Years: From 1900 to the First World War.* New York, 1960.†
20 LUBOVE, Roy. *The Struggle for Social Security, 1900–1935.* Cambridge, Mass., 1968.
21 LUBOVE, Roy. *Progressives and the Slums: Tenement House Reform in New York City, 1890–1917.* Pittsburgh, 1962.

SOCIAL HISTORY AND SOCIETY

1. MOWRY, George E. *The Era of Theodore Roosevelt, 1900–1912.* New York, 1958.†
2. MURRAY, Robert K. *Red Scare: A Study in National Hysteria, 1919–1920.* New York, 1955.†
3. SLOSSON, Preston W. *The Great Crusade and After, 1914–1928.* New York, 1946.
4. SOULE, George. *Prosperity Decade, 1917–1929.* New York, 1947.
5. SULLIVAN, Mark. *Our Times, 1900–1925.* 6 vols. New York, 1926–1935.
6. SWADOS, Harvey. *Years of Conscience—The Muckrakers.* Gloucester, Mass., 1962.†
7. WEINBERG, Arthur M. and Lila, eds. *The Muckrakers, 1902–1912.* New York, 1964.
8. WIEBE, Robert H. *Businessmen and Reform: A Study of the Progressive Movement.* Cambridge, Mass., 1962.

E. Between The Two Wars

9. ADAMS, Samuel H. *Incredible Era: The Life and Times of Warren G. Harding.* New York, 1964.†
10. ALLEN, Frederick Lewis. *Only Yesterday.* New York, 1931.†
11. ALLEN, Frederick Lewis. *Since Yesterday: The Nineteen-Thirties in America, Sept. 3, 1929–Sept. 3, 1939.* New York, 1940.†
12. ALSBERG, H. G., ed. *America Fights the Depression, A Photographic Record of the CWA.* New York, 1934.
13. BEARD, Charles A. and Mary R. *America in Midpassage.* 2 vols. New York, 1939.
14. BIRD, Caroline. *The Invisible Scar: The Great Depression and What It Did to American Life from Then until Now.* New York, 1965.
15. BOARDMAN, Fon W., Jr. *The Thirties: America and the Great Depression.* New York, 1967.
16. BRAEMAN, John et al, eds. *Change and Continuity in Twentieth Century America: the 1920's.* Columbus, Ohio, 1968.
17. CALDWELL, Erskine and Margaret BOURKE-WHITE. *Say! Is this the U.S.A.?* New York, 1941.
18. CHAMBERS, Clarke A. *Seedtime of Reform: American Social Service and Social Action, 1918–1933.* Minneapolis, 1963.†
19. DANIELS, Jonathan. *The Time Between the Wars: Armistice to Pearl Harbor.* Garden City, N.Y., 1966.
20. DERBER, Milton, and Edwin YOUNG, eds. *Labor and the New Deal.* Madison, Wis., 1957.
21. DREISER, Theodore. *American Tragedy.* New York, 1925.†
22. EVANS, Walker. *American Photographs.* New York, 1938.
23. FURNAS, Joseph C. *How America Lives.* New York, 1941.

8 SOCIAL HISTORY AND SOCIETY

1 GALBRAITH, John Kenneth. *The Great Crash, 1929.* Boston, 1955.†
2 GOLDMAN, Eric F. *Rendezvous with Destiny; A History of Modern American Reform.* New York, 1952.†
3 GRAHAM, Otis L., Jr. *An Encore for Reform: The Old Progressives and the New Deal.* New York, 1967.†
4 GREENE, Laurence. *The Era of Wonderful Nonsense.* Indianapolis, 1939.
5 GURKO, Leo. *Angry Decade.* New York, 1947.
6 GUTTMANN, Allen. *The Wound in the Heart: America and the Spanish Civil War.* New York, 1962.
7 HICKS, John D. *Republican Ascendancy, 1921-1933.* New York, 1960.†
8 LANGE, Dorothea, and P. S. TAYLOR. *An American Exodus.* New York, 1939.
9 LEIGHTON, Isabel, ed. *The Aspirin Age, 1919-1941.* New York, 1949.†
10 LEUCHTENBURG, William E. *Franklin D. Roosevelt and the New Deal, 1932-1940.* New York, 1963.†
11 MAC LEISH, Archibald. *Land of the Free.* New York, 1938.
12 MAY, Henry F. "Shifting Perspectives on the 1920's." *Miss Val Hist Rev,* XLIII (1956), 405-427.
13 MITCHELL, Broadus. *Depression Decade; From New Era to New Deal, 1929-1941.* New York, 1947.†
14 MORRIS, Wright. *The Inhibitants.* New York, 1946.
15 MOWRY, George E., ed. *The Twenties: Fords, Flappers and Fanatics.* Englewood Cliffs, N.J., 1963.
16 ROGERS, Agnes, and Frederick Lewis ALLEN. *I Remember Distinctly, a Family Album of the American People, 1918-1941.* New York, 1947.
17 ROMASCO, Albert U. *The Poverty of Abundance: Hoover, the Nation, the Depression.* New York, 1965.†
18 SCHLESINGER, Arthur M., Jr. *The Age of Roosevelt.* 3 vols. Boston, 1957-1961.†
19 SCHRIFTGIESSER, Karl. *This Was Normalcy.* Boston, 1948.
20 SELDES, Gilbert V. *The Years of the Locust: America, 1929-1933.* New York, 1933.
21 SHANNON, David A. *Between the Wars: America, 1919-1941.* Boston, 1965.†
22 SIMON, Rita J., ed. *As We Saw the Thirties.* Urbana, Ill., 1967.
23 SOULE, George. *Prosperity Decade.* See 7.4.
24 STEARNS, Harold, ed. *Civilization in the U.S.* New York, 1922.
25 WARREN, Harris. *Herbert Hoover and the Great Depression.* New York, 1959.
26 WECTER, Dixon. *The Age of the Great Depression, 1929-1941.* New York, 1948.

1 WOOFTER, T. J., and Ellen WINSTON. *Seven Lean Years.* Chapel Hill, 1939.

F. *World War II and the Aftermath*

2 CHASE, John W., ed. *Years of the Modern; an American Appraisal.* New York, 1949.
3 Editors of *Fortune. U.S.A. The Permanent Revolution.* New York, 1951.
4 GOLDMAN, Eric F. *The Crucial Decade—and After: America 1945–1960.* New York, 1961.†
5 GUNTHER, John, and Bernard QUINT. *Days to Remember; America 1945–1955.* New York, 1956.
6 HAVIGHURST, Robert J., and H. Gerthon MORGAN. *Social History of a War Boom Community.* New York, 1951.
7 MAULDIN, Bill. *Back Home.* New York, 1947.
8 MERRILL, Francis E. *Social Problems on the Home Front, A Study of War-Time Influences.* New York, 1948.
9 OGBURN, William F. *American Society in Wartime.* Chicago, 1943.
10 POLENBERG, Richard, comp. *America at War: The Home Front, 1941–1945.* Englewood Cliffs, N.J., 1968.†
11 WECTER, Dixon et al. *Changing Patterns in American Civilization.* Gloucester, Mass., 1949.

G. *The 1950's and 1960's*

12 DEWHURST, James F., and associates. *America's Needs and Resources. A New Survey.* New York, 1955.
13 GETTLEMAN, Marvin E., and David MERMELSTEIN. *The Great Society Reader. The Failure of American Liberalism.* New York, 1967.
14 GOLDMAN, Eric F. *The Crucial Decade—and After: America 1945–1960.* See 9.4.
15 HICKS, Granville. "How We Live Now in America." *Commentary* XVI (Dec. 1953), 505–512.
16 LEWIS, Anthony, and the *New York Times. Portrait of a Decade: The Second American Revolution.* New York, 1964.†
17 WHITNEY, David C. *The Trials and Triumphs of Two Dynamic Decades: A Pictorial History of the Space Age Generation.* Ed. by Thomas C. Jones and Harriet B. Helmer. New York, 1968.

III. The Nation and Its Sections
A. General

1. JENSEN, Merrill, ed. *Regionalism in America.* Madison, Wis., 1951.†
2. O'NEILL, William L. *America Society Since 1945.* Chicago, 1969.
3. STEWART, George R. *Names on the Land: A Historical Account of Place-Naming in the United States.* Boston, 1958.

B. New England (Me., N.H., Vt., Mass., R.I., Conn.)

4. BROOKS, Van Wyck. *New England: Indian Summer.* New York, 1940.†
5. HILL, Ralph N. *Yankee Kingdom.* New York, 1960.
6. HOWE, Helen Huntington. *The Gentle Americans, 1864–1960. Biography of a Breed.* New York, 1965.
7. HOWE, Henry F. *Massachusetts: There She Is—Behold Her.* New York, 1960.
8. HUTHMACHER, J. Joseph *Massachusetts People and Politics, 1919–1933.* Cambridge, Mass., 1959.
9. KIRKLAND, Edward C. *Men, Cities and Transportation: A Study in New England History, 1820–1900.* 2 vols. Cambridge, Mass., 1968.
10. KITTRIDGE, Henry C. *Cape Cod: Its People and Their History.* New York, 1968.
11. RICH, Louise, D. *State o' Maine.* New York, 1964.
12. SOLOMON, Barbara Miller. *Ancestors and Immigrants: A Changing New England Tradition.* Cambridge, Mass., 1956.†

C. The Middle Atlantic States (N.Y., N.J., Pa.)

13. PIERCE, Arthur D. *Iron in the Pines: The Story of New Jersey's Ghost Towns and Bog Iron.* New Brunswick, N.J., 1957.
14. TRACHTENBERG, Alan. *Brooklyn Bridge: Fact and Symbol.* New York, 1965.
15. VECOLI, Rudolph J. *The People of New Jersey.* Princeton, 1965.
16. WALLACE, Paul A. W. *Pennsylvania: Seed of a Nation.* New York, 1962.
17. WARE, Caroline F. *Greenwich Village, 1920–1930.* Boston, 1935.

D. The North Central States (Ohio, Ind., Ill., Mich., Wis.)

18. ATHERTON, Lewis. *Main Street on the Middle Border.* New York, 1954.†

THE NATION AND ITS SECTIONS

1. BOGUE, Allan G. *From Prairie to Corn Belt: Farming on the Illinois and Iowa Prairies in the Nineteenth Century.* Chicago, 1963.†
2. BRITT, Albert. *An America That Was: What Life Was Like on an Illinois Farm Seventy Years Ago.* Barre, Mass. 1964.
3. ESAREY, Logan. *The Indiana Home.* Crawfordsville, Ind., 1953.
4. GLAZER, Sidney. *The Middle West: A Study of Progress.* Detroit, 1962.
5. HELGESON, Arlan. *Farms in the Cutover: Agricultural Settlement in Northern Wisconsin.* Madison, Wis., 1962.
6. HUNKER, Henry L. *Industrial Evolution of Columbus, Ohio.* Columbus, Ohio, 1958.
7. JORDAN, Philip D. "Ohio Comes of Age: 1873–1900." Vol. V of *The History of the State of Ohio.* Ed. by Carl Wittke. Columbus, Ohio, 1944.
8. LANDON, Fred. *Lake Huron.* Indianapolis, 1944.
9. MAY, George S. *Pictorial History of Michigan: The Early Years.* Grand Rapids, Mich., 1967.
10. NUTE, Grace L. *Lake Superior.* Minneapolis, 1944.
11. PEASE, Theodore C. *The Story of Illinois.* Chicago, 1965.
12. POUND, Arthur. *Lake Ontario.* Indianapolis, 1945.
13. QUAIFE, Milo M. *Lake Michigan.* Indianapolis, 1944.
14. ROSEBOOM, Eugene H. "The Civil War Era, 1850–1873." Vol. IV of *The History of the State of Ohio.* Ed. by Carl Wittke. Columbus, Ohio, 1944.
15. ROSEBOOM, Eugene H., and Francise P. WEISENBURGER. *A History of Ohio.* Ed. and illus. by James H. Rodabaugh. Columbus, Ohio, 1953.
16. SANTMYER, Helen H. *Ohio Town.* Columbus, Ohio, 1962.
17. WELLER, Jack E. *Yesterday's People: Life in Contemporary Appalachia.* Lexington, Ky. 1965.
18. WILSON, William E. *Indiana: A History.* Bloomington, 1966.
19. WOODFORD, Frank B. and Arthur M. *All Our Yesterdays: A Brief History of Detroit.* Detroit, 1969.†

E. *The Border States (Del., Md., D.C., W.Va., Ky., Tenn.)*

20. AMBLER, Charles H., and Festus P. SUMMERS. *West Virginia: The Mountain State.* New York, 1958.
21. CAMPBELL, John C. *The Southern Highlander and His Homeland.* New York, 1921.†
22. CAUDILL, Harry M. *Night Comes to the Cumberlands.* Boston, 1963.
23. CLAPP, Gordon R. *The TVA: An Approach to the Development of a Region.* Chicago, 1955.

1. CLARK, Thomas D. *Kentucky, Land of Contrast.* New York, 1968.
2. DUFFUS, Robert Luther. *The Valley and Its People, a Portrait of TVA.* New York, 1944.
3. FOLMSBEE, Stanley J. et al. *Tennessee: A Short History.* Knoxville, Tenn., 1969.†
4. GREEN, Constance McLaughlin. *Washington.* 2 vols. Princeton, 1962–1963.

F. The Southern States (Va., N.C., S.C., Ga., Fla., Ala., Miss., Ark., La.)

5. AGEE, James, and Walker EVANS. *Let Us Now Praise Famous Men.* New York, 1941; 1960.†
6. BERTELSON, David. *The Lazy South.* New York, 1967.
7. BETTERSWORTH, John K. *Mississippi: Yesterday and Today.* New York, 1964.
8. BRANDFON, Robert L., comp. *The American South in the Twentieth Century.* New York, 1967.†
9. BRANDFON, Robert L. *Cotton Kingdom of the New South: A History of the Yazoo Mississippi Delta from Reconstruction to the Twentieth Century.* Cambridge, Mass., 1967.
10. CASH, Wilbur J. *The Mind of the South.* New York, 1960.†
11. CLARK, Thomas D. *The Emerging South.* New York, 1961.
12. CLARK, Thomas D. *Pills, Petticoats, and Plows: The Southern Country Store.* New York, 1964.
13. CLARK, Thomas D. *The Rural Press and the New South.* Baton Rouge, 1948.
14. CLARK, Thomas D. *The Southern Country Editor.* Indianapolis, 1948.
15. CLARK, Thomas D., ed. *Bluegrass Cavalcade.* Lexington, Ky., 1956.
16. CLARK, Thomas D., and Albert D. KIRWAN. *The South since Appomattox: A Century of Regional Change.* New York, 1967.
17. COULTER, E. Merton. *Wormsloe: Two Centuries of a Georgia Family.* Athens, Ga., 1955.
18. CUNNINGHAM, Horace H. *The Southern Mind Since the Civil War.* Baton Rouge, 1965.
19. DAVIDSON, Donald et al. *I'll Take My Stand. The South and the Agrarian Tradition by 12 Southerners.* New York, 1930.
20. DAVIS, Allison, et al. *Deep South.* Chicago, 1941.
21. DAVIS, Edwin A. *Louisiana—The Pelican State.* 3d edition. Baton Rouge, 1969.
22. DOLLARD, John. *Caste and Class in a Southern Town.* New Haven, 1937.

1 DOUGLAS, Marjory S. *Florida: The Long Frontier.* New York, 1967.
2 DUFOUR, Charles L. *Ten Flags in the Wind: The Story of Louisiana.* New York, 1967.
3 DYKEMAN, Wilma, and James STOKELY. *Seeds of Southern Change: The Life of Will Alexander.* Chicago, 1962.
4 FISHWICK, Marshall W. *Virginia: A New Look at the Old Dominion.* New York, 1959.
5 GRANTHAM, Dewey W., Jr. *The Democratic South.* Athens, Ga., 1963.†
6 GRANTHAM, Dewey W., Jr. *The Twentieth Century South.* Athens, Ga., 1966.
7 LANDER, Ernest M. *A History of South Carolina, 1865-1960.* Chapel Hill, 1960.
8 LEFLER, Hugh T., and Albert R. NEWSOME. *North Carolina: The History of a Southern State.* Chapel Hill, 1963.
9 Mc GILL, Ralph. *The South and the Southerner.* Boston, 1963.†
10 MARSHALL, F. Ray. *Labor in the South.* Cambridge, Mass., 1967.
11 POTWIN, Marjorie A. *Cotton Mill People of the Piedmont.* New York, 1927.
12 QUINT, Howard H. *Profile in Black and White: A Frank Portrait of South Carolina.* Washington, D.C., 1958.
13 SHUGG, R. W. *Origins of Class Struggle in Louisiana.* Baton Rouge, 1968.†
14 SIMKINS, Francis B. *A History of the South.* New York, 1963.
15 SMEDES, Susan D. *Memorials of a Southern Planter.* Ed. by Fletcher M. Green. New York, 1965.
16 THOMPSON, Lawrence S. *Foreign Travellers in the South, 1900-1950.* Rochester, 1954.
17 TINDALL, George Brown. *The Emergence of the New South, 1913-1945.* Baton Rouge, 1967.
18 WALLACE, David D. *South Carolina, A Short History, 1520-1948.* Columbia, S.C., 1951.
19 WOODWARD, C. Vann. *Origins of the New South, 1877-1913.* See 6.8.
20 ZINN, Howard. *The Southern Mystique.* Boston, 1964.†

G. The West

1. GENERAL

21 BILLINGTON, Ray Allen. *The Far Western Frontier 1830-1860.* New York, 1956.†
22 BROWN, Dee. *The Gentle Tamers: Women in the Old Wild West.* Lincoln, Neb., 1958.†

14 THE NATION AND ITS SECTIONS

1 CURTI, Merle. *The Making of an American Community: A Case Study of Democracy in a Frontier County.* Stanford, 1959.†
2 DALE, Edward E. *Frontier Way: Sketches of Life in the Old West.* Philadelphia, 1959.
3 DICK, Everett. *The Sod-House Frontier, 1854–1890.* Lincoln, Neb., 1950.
4 DYKSTRA, Robert R. *The Cattle Towns.* New York, 1968.
5 FUSSELL, Edwin. *Frontier: American Literature and the American West.* Princeton, 1965.
6 GREEVER, William S. *The Bonanza West: The Story of the Western Mining Rushes, 1848–1900.* Norman, Okla., 1963.
7 HAWGOOD, John A. *America's Western Frontiers: The Exploration and Settlement of the Trans-Mississippi West.* New York, 1967.
8 LAVENDER, David. *The American Heritage History of the Great West.* Ed. by Alvin M. Josephy and Ralph K. Andrist. New York, 1965.
9 MOODY, Ralph. *Stagecoach West.* New York, 1967.
10 MORGAN, Dale L., ed. *Rand McNally's Pioneer Atlas of the American West.* Chicago, 1956.
11 PADEN, Irene D. *The Wake of the Prairie Schooner.* New York, 1943.
12 POMEROY, Earl. *In Search of the Golden West: The Tourist in Western America.* New York, 1957.
13 SHARP, Paul F. *Whoop-up Country: The Canadian-American West, 1865–1885.* Butte, Mont., 1960.
14 TAFT, Robert. *Artists and Illustrators of the Old West, 1850–1900.* New York, 1953.
15 TILDEN, Freeman. *Following the Frontier with F. Jay Haynes, Pioneer Photographer of the Old West.* New York, 1964.
16 VANORMAN, Richard A. *A Room for the Night: Hotels of the Old West.* Bloomington, 1966.
17 WEBB, Walter P. *The Great Frontier.* Austin, Tex., 1964.
18 WINTHER, Oscar O. *The Transportation Frontier: Trans-Mississippi West, 1865–1890.* New York, 1964.

2. *THE GREAT PLAINS STATES (MINN., IOWA, MO., N.D., S.D., KAN., NEB., OKLA., TEX.)*

19 ANDERSON, George L. *Kansas West.* San Marino, Calif., 1963.
20 ATHEARN, Robert G. *High Country Empire: The High Plains and Rockies.* Lincoln, Neb., 1960.†
21 BAINBRIDGE, John. *The Super-Americans; A Picture of Life in The United States . . . in the Land of The Millionaires—Texas.* Garden City, N.Y., 1961.
22 BARNES, Cass G. *The Sod House.* Lincoln, Nebr., 1970.†

THE NATION AND ITS SECTIONS

1 BOGUE, Margaret B. *Patterns from the Sod: Land Use and Tenure in the Grand Prairie, 1850–1900.* Springfield, Ill., 1959.
2 BROWN, A. Theodore. *Frontier Community: Kansas City to 1870.* Columbia, Mo., 1963.
3 BROWN, Mark H., and W. R. FELTON. *The Frontier Years: L. A. Huffman, Photographer of the Plains.* New York, 1955.
4 DEBO, Angie. *Prairie City: The Story of an American Community.* New York, 1944.
5 FIELD, Matthew C. *Prairie and Mountain Sketches.* Ed. by Kate L. Gregg and John F. McDermott. New York, 1957.
6 GARD, Wayne. *The Great Buffalo Hunt.* Lincoln, Neb., 1959.†
7 HART, Henry C. *The Dark Missouri.* Madison, Wis., 1957.
8 HEILBRON, Bertha L. *The Thirty-Second State: A Pictorial History of Minnesota.* St. Paul, Minn., 1966.
9 HOLLON, W. Eugene. *The Great American Desert: Then and Now.* New York, 1966.
10 HOLLON, W. Eugene. *Rushing for Land: Oklahoma 1889.* Norman, Okla., 1966.
11 LAVENDER, David. *Bent's Fort.* New York, 1954.
12 LUEBKE, Frederick C. *Immigrants and Politics: The Germans of Nebraska, 1880–1900.* Lincoln, Nebr., 1969.
13 Mc REYNOLDS, Edwin C. *Missouri: A History of the Crossroads State.* Norman, Okla., 1962.
14 Mc REYNOLDS, Edwin C. et al. *Oklahoma; The Story of Its Past and Present.* Norman, Okla., 1961.
15 MALIN, James C. *The Grasslands of North America.* New York, 1967.
16 MILLER, Nyle H. et al. *Kansas: A Pictorial History.* Topeka, Kan., 1961.
17 NICOLL, Bruce H. *Nebraska: A Pictorial History.* Lincoln, Neb., 1967.
18 OLSON, James C. *History of Nebraska.* Lincoln, Neb., 1955.
19 PRETTYMAN, W. S. *Indian Territory: A Frontier Photographic Record.* Ed. by Robert E. Cunningham. Norman, Okla., 1957.
20 RISTER, Carl C. *No Man's Land.* Norman, Okla., 1948.
21 ROBINSON, Elwyn B. *History of North Dakota.* Lincoln, Neb., 1966.
22 SANDOZ, Mari. *Old Jules.* New York, 1955.†
23 SCHELL, Herbert S. *History of South Dakota.* Lincoln, Neb., 1961.
24 WEBB, Walter P. *The Great Plains.* Boston, 1959.†
25 WEST, James C. W. *Plainville, U.S.A.* New York, 1945.†
26 ZORNOW, William Frank. *Kansas: A History of the Jayhawk State.* Norman, Okla., 1957.

3. THE MOUNTAIN STATES (MONT., IDAHO, WYO., COLO., N. MEX., ARIZ., UTAH, NEV.)

1 ALLEN, James B. *The Company Town in the American West.* New York, 1966.
2 ATHEARN, Robert G. *High Country Empire.* See 14.20.
3 BECK, Warren A. *New Mexico: A History of Four Centuries.* New York, 1962.
4 FAULK, Odie B. *Land of Many Frontiers: A History of the American Southwest.* New York, 1968.
5 HOWARD, Joseph K. *Montana: High, Wide, and Handsome.* New Haven, 1959.
6 LARSON, Taft A. *History of Wyoming.* Lincoln, Neb., 1965.
7 LILLARD, Richard G. *Desert Challenge: An Interpretation of Nevada.* Lincoln, Neb., 1966.†
8 MORGAN, Dale L. *The Great Salt Lake.* Indianapolis, 1947.
9 OSTRANDER, Gilman M. *Nevada, The Great Rotten Borough, 1859–1964.* New York, 1966.
10 POWELL, John Wesley. *Report on the Lands of the Arid Region of the United States, with a More Detailed Account of the Lands of Utah.* Ed. by Wallace Stegner. Cambridge, Mass., 1962.
11 STEGNER, Wallace. *Beyond the Hundredth Meridian: John Wesley Powell and the Second Opening of the West.* New York, 1954.†
12 STEGNER, Wallace. *The Gathering of Zion: The Story of the Mormon Trail.* New York, 1964.
13 TOOLE, K. Ross. *Montana: An Uncommon Land.* Norman, Okla., 1959.

4. THE PACIFIC STATES (WASH., ORE., CALIF., ALASKA, HAWAII)

14 ADAMS, Ben. *The Last Frontier: A Short History of Alaska.* New York, 1961.
15 BEAN, Walton E. *California: An Interpretive History.* New York, 1968.
16 BRIGGS, Harold E. *Frontiers of the Northwest.* New York, 1940.
17 CAUGHEY, John W. *California.* 2d ed. New York, 1953.
18 DAMON, Ethel M. *Sanford Dallard Dole and His Hawaii.* Palo Alto, Calif., 1957.
19 DAWS, Gavin. *Shoal of Time: A History of the Hawaiian Islands.* New York, 1968.
20 DAY, A. Grove. *Hawaii and Its People.* Brattleboro, Vt., 1968.
21 GRUENING, Ernest. *The State of Alaska.* New York, 1968.
22 HULLEY, Clarence C. *Alaska, Past and Present.* Portland, Ore., 1953.

1. JOHANSEN, Dorothy O., and Charles M. GATES. *Empire of the Columbia: A History of the Pacific Northwest.* New York, 1967.
2. MAC MULLEN, Jerry. *Paddle-Wheel Days in California.* Stanford, 1944.
3. MC WILLIAMS, Carey, ed. *The California Revolution.* New York, 1968.
4. POMEROY, Earl. *The Pacific Slope: A History of California, Oregon, Washington, Idaho, Utah, and Nevada.* New York, 1965.
5. ROLLE, Andrew F. *California: A History.* New York, 1963.
6. RUSS, William A., Jr. *The Hawaiian Republic (1894–98) and Its Struggle to Win Annexation.* Selinsgrove, Pa., 1961.
7. SCOTT, Meliero G. *The San Francisco Bay Area: A Metropolis in Perspective.* Berkeley, 1959.
8. VAUGHAN, Thomas, and Priscilla KNUTH. *A Bibliography of Pacific Northwest History.* Portland, Ore., 1958.

IV. The Rise of the City

9. ADDAMS, Jane. *Twenty Years at Hull House.* See 6.10.
10. BEIRNE, Francis F. *Baltimore: A Picture History.* New York, 1957.
11. BLAKE, Nelson M. *Water for the Cities.* Syracuse, 1956.
12. BUDER, Stanley. *Pullman: An Experiment in Industrial Order and Community Planning 1890–1930.* New York, 1967.
13. CROSS, Robert D., ed. *The Church and the City, 1865–1910.* Indianapolis, 1966.†
14. DAHL, Robert A. *Who Governs? Democracy and Power in an American City.* New Haven, 1961.†
15. DEGLER, Carl N. "American Political Parties and the Rise of the City: An Interpretation." *Miss Val Hist Rev,* LI (1964), 41–59.
16. ELDREDGE, H. Wentworth. *Taming Megalopolis.* 2 vols. New York, 1967.†
17. FOGELSON, Robert M. *The Fragmented Metropolis: Los Angeles, 1850–1930.* Cambridge, Mass., 1967.
18. GANS, Herbert. *The Levittowners: Ways of Life and Politics in a New Suburban Community.* New York, 1967.†
19. GINGER, Ray. *Modern American Cities.* Chicago, 1969.
20. GLAAB, Charles N., and A. Theodore BROWN. *A History of Urban America.* New York, 1967.†
21. GLAZER, Nathan, and Daniel P. MOYNIHAN. *Beyond the Melting Pot.* Cambridge, Mass., 1963.†
22. GOODALL, Leonard E. *The American Metropolis.* Columbus, Ohio, 1967.†

1 GOODMAN, Paul and Percival. *Communities, Means of Livelihood and Ways of Life.* New York, 1958.†
2 GOTTMAN, Jean. *Megalopolis: The Urbanized Northeastern Seaboard of the United States.* New York, 1961.†
3 GREEN, Constance McLaughlin. *American Cities in the Growth of the Nation.* New York, 1957.
4 GREEN, Constance McLaughlin. *The Rise of Urban America.* New York, 1965.†
5 GREEN, Constance McLaughlin. *Washington.* See 12.4.
6 HANDLIN, Oscar, and John BURCHARD, eds. *The Historian and the City.* Cambridge, Mass., 1963.†
7 HAUSER, Philip M., and Leo F. SCHNORE, eds. *The Study of Urbanization.* New York, 1965.
8 HOLLI, Melvin G. *Reform in Detroit; Hazen S. Pingree and Urban Politics.* New York, 1959.
9 HOOVER, Edgar M., and Raymond VERNON. *Anatomy of a Metropolis.* New York, 1962.
10 HUNGERFORD, Edward. *Personality of American Cities.* New York, 1913.
11 HUNTER, David R. *The Slums: Challenge and Response.* New York, 1968.
12 HUTHMACHER, J. Joseph. "Urban Liberalism and the Age of Reform." *Miss Val Hist Rev,* XLIX (1962), 231–241.
13 JACKSON, Joy J. *New Orleans in The Gilded Age: Politics and Urban Progress, 1880–1896.* Baton Rouge, 1969.
14 JACOBS, Jane. *The Death and Life of Great American Cities.* New York, 1961.†
15 KANE, Lucile M. *The Waterfall That Built a City: The Falls of St. Anthony in Minneapolis.* St. Paul, Minn., 1966.
16 KELLOGG, Paul U., ed. *The Pittsburgh Survey.* 6 vols. New York, 1907–1914.
17 KOUWENHOVEN, John A. *The Columbia Historical Portrait of New York,* Garden City, N.Y., 1953.
18 LANE, Roger. *Policing the City: Boston 1822–1885.* Cambridge, Mass., 1967.
19 LORANT, Stefan. *Pittsburgh: The Story of an American City.* New York, 1964.
20 LOWE, Jeanne R. *Cities in a Race with Time: Progress and Poverty in America's Renewing Cities.* New York, 1967.†
21 Mc KELVEY, Blake. *The Emergence of Metropolitan America, 1915–1966.* New Brunswick, N.J., 1968.
22 Mc KELVEY, Blake. *Rochester.* Vols. II, III and IV. Cambridge, Mass., 1949–1961.
23 Mc KELVEY, Blake. *The Urbanization of America, 1860–1915.* New Brunswick, N.J., 1963.

THE RISE OF THE CITY

1. MANDELBAUM, Seymour J. *Boss Tweed's New York.* New York, 1965.
2. MARX, Leo. *The Machine in the Garden.* New York, 1964.†
3. MAYER, Grace M. *Once Upon a City.* New York, 1958.
4. MAYER, Harold M., and Richard C. WADE, with the assistance of Glen E. Holt. *Chicago: Growth of a Metropolis.* Chicago, 1969.
5. MILLER, William D. *Memphis During the Progressive Era, 1900-1917.* Memphis, Tenn., 1957.
6. MILLER, William L. *The Fifteenth Ward and the Great Society; An Encounter with a Modern City.* Boston, 1966.
7. MILLER, Zane L. *Boss Cox's Cincinnati: Urban Politics in the Progressive Era.* New York, 1968.
8. MOWRY, George. *The Urban Nation, 1920-1960.* New York, 1965.†
9. MUMFORD, Lewis. *Culture of Cities,* New York, 1938.
10. NEVINS, Allan. *Emergence of Modern America.* See 4.19.
11. OSTERWEIS, Rollin G. *Three Centuries of New Haven, 1638-1938.* New Haven, 1953.
12. PIERCE, Bessie L. *History of Chicago.* 3 vols., New York, 1937-1957.
13. REPS, John W. *The Making of Urban America: A History of City Planning in the United States.* Princeton, 1965.
14. RIIS, Jacob A. *How the Other Half Lives.* New York, 1890; 1959.†
15. SCHLESINGER, Arthur M. *The Rise of the City, 1878-1898.* New York, 1933.
16. SCHMITT, Peter J. *Back to Nature: The Arcadian Myth in Urban America.* New York, 1969.
17. SMITH, Page. *As a City Upon a Hill: The Town in American History.* New York, 1966.
18. STILL, Bayrd. *Milwaukee: The History of a City.* Madison, Wis., 1965.
19. STILL, Bayrd. *Mirror for Gotham: New York as Seen by Contemporaries from Dutch Days to the Present.* New York, 1956.
20. SYRETT, Harold C. *The City of Brooklyn 1865-1898: A Political History.* New York, 1944.
21. TAGER, Jack. *The Intellectual as Urban Reformer; Brand Whitlock and the Progressive Movement.* Cleveland, 1968.
22. TATUM, George B. *Penn's Great Town, 250 Years of Philadelphia Architecture Illustrated in Prints and Drawings.* Philadelphia, 1961.
23. THERNSTROM, Stephan, and Richard SENNETT, eds. *Nineteenth Century Cities: Essays in The New Urban History.* New Haven, 1969.
24. TUNNARD, Christopher, and H. H. REED. *American Skyline; The Growth and Form of our Cities and Towns.* New York, 1956.†
25. TUNNARD, Christopher. *The City of Man.* New York, 1953.

1. WARNER, Sam Bass, Jr., *Streetcar Suburbs: The Process of Growth in Boston, 1870–1900*. Cambridge, Mass., 1962.†
2. WARNER, Sam Bass, Jr. *The Private City: Philadelphia in Three Periods of Its Growth.* Philadelphia, 1968.
3. WARNER, Sam Bass, Jr., ed. *Planning for a Nation of Cities.* Cambridge, Mass., 1967.†
4. WARNER, William Lloyd and Paul S. HUNT. *The Social Life of a Modern Community.* New Haven, 1941.
5. WHITE, Morton and Lucia. *The Intellectual Versus the City.* Cambridge, Mass., 1962.
6. WHITEHILL, Walter M. *Boston: A Topographical History.* Cambridge, Mass., 1968.
7. WHYTE, William I. *Streetcorner Society: The Social Structure of an Italian Slum.* 2d ed. Chicago, 1955.
8. WOOD, Robert C. *Suburbia: Its People and Their Politics.* New York, 1959.
9. ZORBAUGH, Harvey. *Gold Coast and Slum.* Chicago, 1929.

V. The American People

A. Population and General Works (including contemporary social surveys)

10. CHARLESWORTH, James C., ed. "The Changing American People: Are We Deteriorating or Improving?" *Ann Am Acad Pol Soc Sci*, CCCLXXVIII (1968).
11. DAY, Lincoln H., and Alice Taylor DAY. *Too Many Americans.* New York, 1965.†
12. ELDRIDGE, Hope T., and Dorothy Swaine THOMAS. *Population Redistribution and Economic Growth, United States, 1870–1950.* Vol. III. New York, 1964.
13. GRABILL, Wilson H. et al. *The Fertility of American Women.* New York, 1958.
14. HANDLIN, Oscar. *The American People in the Twentieth Century.* Cambridge, Mass., 1954.†
15. HAUSER, Philip M. *Population Perspectives.* New Brunswick, N.J., 1962.
16. LEE, Everett S. et al. *Population Redistribution and Economic Growth, United States, 1870–1950.* Vol. I. New York, 1957.
17. LYND, Robert S., and Helen M. *Middletown.* Cambridge, Mass., 1929.†
18. MURDOCK, G. P. *Ethnographic Bibliography of North America.* 3d ed. New Haven, 1960.
19. OKUN, Bernard. *Trends in Birth Rates in the United States Since 1870.* Baltimore, 1958.

THE AMERICAN PEOPLE 21

1 SHELDON, Henry D. *The Older Population of the United States.* New York, 1958.
2 STOCKWELL, Edward G. *Population and People.* Chicago, 1968.
3 TAEUBER, Conrad and Irene B. *The Changing Population of the United States.* New York, 1958.
4 TRACY, Stanley J., ed. *A Report on World Population Migration as Related to the United States of America.* Washington, D.C., 1956.
5 U.S. Bureau of the Census. *Statistical Abstract of the United States.* Washington, D.C., 1878–present.
6 WATTENBERG, Ben J., and Richard M. SCAMMON. *This U.S.A.: An Unexpected Family Portrait of 194,067,296 Americans Drawn from the Census.* New York, 1965.†

B. Social Classes and Social Mobility

7 AMORY, Cleveland. *Who Killed Society?* New York, 1960.
8 BALTZELL, E. Digby. *Philadelphia Gentlemen: The Making of a National Upper Class.* Glencoe, Ill, 1958.†
9 BIRMINGHAM, Stephen. *The Right People: A Portrait of the American Social Establishment.* Boston, 1968.
10 BLAW, Peter Michael and Duncan. *The American Occupational Structure.* New York, 1967.
11 COMMAGER, Henry Steele. "Do We have a Class Society." *Va Q Rev* XXXVII (1961), 548–557.
12 KELLER, Suzanne. *Beyond the Ruling Class: Strategic Elites in Modern Society.* New York, 1963.
13 KOLKO, Gabriel. *Wealth and Power in America: Analysis of Social Class and Income Distribution.* New York, 1962.†
14 LIPSET, Seymour Martin, and Reinhard BENDIX. *Social Mobility in Industrial Society.* Berkeley, 1959.†
15 MILLS, C. Wright. *The Power Elite.* New York, 1956.†
16 MILLS, C. Wright. *White Collar. The American Middle Classes.* New York, 1951.†
17 PETERSEN, William. "Is America Still the Land of Opportunity: What Recent Studies Show About Social Mobility." *Commentary,* XVI (1953), 477–486.
18 REISSMAN, Leonard. *Class in American Society.* Glencoe, Ill., 1959.†
19 TEBBEL, John William. *The Inheritors: a Study of America's Great Fortunes and What Happened to Them.* New York, 1962.
20 THERNSTROM, Stephan. *Poverty and Progress: Social Mobility in a Nineteenth Century City.* Cambridge, Mass., 1964.†
21 WECTER, Dixon. *The Saga of American Society.* New York, 1937.
22 WILLIAMS, Robin M., Jr. *American Society. A Sociological Interpretation.* 2d ed. New York, 1960.

1 WOLFE, Tom. *The Pump House Gang.* New York, 1968.
2 WYLLIE, Irvin G. *The Self-Made Man in America.* New Brunswick, N.J., 1954.

C. Internal Migration

3 BOGUE, Donald J. et al. *Subregional Migration in the United States, 1935–40.* Vol. 1. Oxford, Ohio, 1957.
4 KUZNETS, Simon et al. *Population Redistribution and Economic Growth, United States, 1870–1950.* 3 vols. Philadelphia, 1957–1964.
5 SMITH, Timothy Lynn. "The Redistribution of the Negro Population of the United States, 1910–1960." *J Neg Hist*, LI (1966), 155–173.

D. Immigration

1. GENERAL

6 ADAMIC, Louis. *A Nation of Nations.* New York, 1945.
7 ANDER, Oscar Fritiof, ed. *In the Trek of the Immigrants: Essays Presented to Carl Wittke.* Rock Island, Ill., 1964.
8 COLE, Donald B. *Immigrant City: Lawrence, Massachusetts, 1845–1921.* Chapel Hill, 1963.
9 COMMAGER, Henry Steele, ed. *Immigration and American History: Essays in Honor of Theodore C. Blegen.* Minneapolis, 1961.
10 DAVIE, M. R. *World Immigration with Special Reference to the United States.* New York, 1936.
11 DIVINE, Robert A. *American Immigration Policy, 1924–1952.* New Haven, 1957.
12 ERICKSON, Charlotte. *American Industry and the European Immigrant, 1860–1885.* Cambridge, Mass., 1957.
13 FERMI, Laura. *Illustrious Immigrants: The Intellectual Migration from Europe, 1930–41.* Chicago, 1968.
14 FLEMING, Donald, and Bernard BAILYN, eds. *The Intellectual Migration: Europe and America, 1930–1960.* Cambridge, Mass., 1968.
15 GLAZER, Nathan, and Daniel P. MOYNIHAN. *Beyond the Melting Pot.*† See 17.21.
16 HANDLIN, Oscar. *Boston's Immigrants: A Study in Acculturation.* Cambridge, Mass., 1959.†
17 HANDLIN, Oscar. *Children of the Uprooted.* New York, 1966.†
18 HANDLIN, Oscar. *Race and Nationality in American Life.* Boston, 1957.†
19 HANDLIN, Oscar, ed. *Immigration as a Factor in American History.* New York, 1959.†

1 HANDLIN, Oscar. *The Uprooted: The Epic Story of the Great Migrations that Made the American People.* Boston, 1951.†
2 HANSEN, Marcus Lee. *The Immigrant in American History.* Ed. by Arthur Schlesinger. New York, 1963.†
3 HARTMANN, Edward George. *The Movement to Americanize the Immigrant.* New York, 1948.
4 HIGHAM, John. *Strangers in the Land: Patterns of American Nativism, 1860–1925.* New York, 1955.†
5 HUTCHINSON, Edward P. *Immigrants and Their Children, 1850–1950.* New York, 1956.
6 JONES, Maldwyn A. *American Immigration.* Chicago, 1960.†
7 RIIS, Jacob A. *The Making of an American.* New York, 1901; 1966.
8 SCHOENER, Allon, ed. *Portal to America: The Lower East Side, 1870–1925.* New York, 1967.
9 SMITH, Timothy Lynn. "New Approaches to the History of Immigration in Twentieth Century America." *Am Hist Rev,* LXXI (1966), 1265–1279.
10 SOLOMON, Barbara Miller. *Ancestors and Immigrants: A Changing New England Tradition.* See 10.12.
11 STEPHENSON, George M. *A History of American Immigration, 1820–1924.* New York, 1926.
12 WIRTH, Louis. *The Ghetto.* Chicago, 1928.†
13 WITTKE, Carl. *We Who Built America.* Cleveland, 1939.†

2. SCANDINAVIA (NORWAY, SWEDEN, DENMARK, FINLAND)

14 ANDER, Oscar Fritiof. *The Cultural Heritage of the Swedish Immigrant: Selected References.* Rock Island, Ill., 1956.
15 BERGMANN, Leola Nelson. *Americans From Norway.* Philadelphia, 1950.
16 BLEGEN, Theodore C. *Norwegian Migration to America.* 2 vols. Northfield, Minn., 1931–1940.
17 HOGLUND, A. William. *Finnish Immigrants in America, 1880–1920.* Madison, Wis., 1960.
18 KOLEHMAINEN, John I., and George W. HILL. *Haven in the Woods: The Story of the Finns in Wisconsin.* Madison, Wis., 1951.
19 MOBERG, Wilhelm. *The Emigrants.* New York, 1951.
20 MULDER, William. *Homeward to Zion: The Mormon Migration from Scandinavia.* Minneapolis, 1957.
21 QUALEY, Carlton C. *Norwegian Settlement in the United States.* New York, 1938.
22 RAAEN, Aagot. *Grass of the Earth: Immigrant Life in the Dakota Country.* Northfield, Minn., 1950.

3. UNITED KINGDOM (ENGLAND, SCOTLAND, WALES, IRELAND)

1. BERTHOFF, Rowland Tappan. *British Immigrants in Industrial America, 1790–1950.* Cambridge, Mass., 1953.

2. CONWAY, Alan, ed. *The Welsh in America: Letters from the Immigrants.* Minneapolis, 1961.

3. HARTMANN, Edward George. *Americans from Wales.* North Quincy, Mass., 1967.

4. LEYBURN, James G. *The Scotch-Irish: A Social History.* Chapel Hill, 1962.

5. SCHRIER, Arnold. *Ireland and the American Emigration, 1850–1900.* Minneapolis, 1958.

6. SHANNON, William. *American Irish.* New York, 1966.

7. SHEPPERSON, Wilbur S. *British Emigration to North America.* Minneapolis, 1957.

8. WINTHER, Oscar O. "English Migration to the American West, 1865–1900." *Hunt Lib Q*, XXVII (1964), 159–173.

9. WITTKE, Carl. *The Irish in America.* Baton Rouge, La., 1956.†

4. WESTERN EUROPE (FRANCE, GERMANY, NETHERLANDS, SWITZERLAND)

10. CUNZ, Dieter. *The Maryland Germans: A History.* Princeton, 1948.

11. LUCAS, Henry S. *Netherlands in America: Dutch Immigration to the United States and Canada, 1789–1950.* Ann Arbor, Mich., 1955.

12. WALKER, Mack. *Germany and the Emigration of 1816–1885.* New York, 1964.

13. WITTKE, Carl. *The German-Language Press in America.* Lexington, Ky., 1957.

14. WITTKE, Carl. "The Germans of Cincinnati." *Bull Hist Philos Soc Ohio*, XX, No. 1 (Jan. 1962), 3–14.

5. SOUTHERN EUROPE (ITALY, GREECE)

15. DORE, Grazia. "Some Social and Historical Aspects of Italian Immigration to America." *J Soc Hist*, II (1968–69), 95–122.

16. FAIRCHILD, Henry Pratt. *Greek Immigration to the United States.* New Haven, 1911.

17. FOERSTER, Robert Franz. *The Italian Immigration of Our Times.* Cambridge, Mass., 1919.

18. GANS, Herbert. *The Urban Villagers: Group and Class in the Life of Italian Americans.* New York, 1962.

19. ROBERTS, Peter. *New Immigration.* New York, 1912.

1 SALOUTOS, Theodore. *The Greeks in the United States.* Cambridge, Mass., 1964.

2 SALOUTOS, Theodore. *They Remember America: The Story of the Repatriated Greek-Americans.* Berkeley, 1956.

3 VECOLI, Rudolph J. "Prelates and Peasants: Italian Immigrants and the Catholic Church." *J Soc Hist,* II (1968–69), 217–268.

6. EASTERN-CENTRAL EUROPE (POLAND, HUNGARY, YUGOSLAVIA)

4 CAPEK, Thomas. *The Czecks (Bohemians) in America.* Boston, 1920.

5 GOVORCHIN, Gerald Gilbert. *Americans from Yugoslavia.* Gainesville, Fla., 1961.

6 KONNYU, Leslie. *Hungarians in the United States; An Immigration Study.* St. Louis, Mo., 1967.†

7 NAPOLSKA, Sister Mary Remigia, O.S.F. *The Polish Immigrant in Detroit to 1914.* Chicago, 1946.

8 SOUDERS, David Aaron. *The Magyars in America.* New York, 1922.

9 THOMAS, W. I., and Florian ZNANIECKI. *The Polish Peasant in Europe and America.* 5 vols. Boston, 1918–20.

10 WYTRWAL, Joseph A. *America's Polish Heritage: A Social History of the Poles in America.* Detroit, 1961.

7. THE ORIENT (CHINA, JAPAN)

11 BARTH, Gunther. *Bitter Strength: A History of the Chinese in the United States, 1850–1870.* Cambridge, Mass., 1964.

12 CHIU, Ping. *Chinese Labor in California, 1850–1880: An Economic Study.* Madison, Wis., 1963.

13 DILLON, Richard H. *The Hatchet Men: The Story of the Tong Wars in San Francisco's Chinatown.* New York, 1962.

14 KUNG, S. W. *Chinese in American Life: Some Aspects of Their History, Status, Problems, and Contributions.* Seattle, 1962.

15 LEE, Rose Hum. *The Chinese in the United States of America.* Hong Kong, 1960.

16 LIND, Andrew W. *Hawaii's Japanese.* Princeton, 1946.

17 Mc WILLIAMS, Carey. *Prejudice: Japanese-Americans: Symbol of Racial Intolerance.* Boston, 1944.

18 MEARS, E. G. *Resident Orientals on the American Pacific Coast.* Chicago, 1928.

19 SEWARD, G. F. *Chinese Immigration in Its Social and Economic Aspects.* New York, 1881.

20 SUNG, Betty Lee. *Mountain of Gold: The Story of the Chinese in America.* New York, 1967.

21 YUAN, D. Y. "Chinatown and Beyond: The Chinese Population in Metropolitan New York." *Phylon,* XXVII (1966), 321–332.

8. THE AMERICAS

1   ALVAREZ, Hernandez. "A Demographic Profile of the Mexican Immigration to the United States, 1910–1950." *J Inter-am Stud*, VIII (1966), 471–496.
2   BURMA, John H. *Spanish-Speaking Groups in the United States*. Durham, N.C., 1954.
3   GAMIO, Manuel. *The Mexican Immigrant, His Life Story*. Chicago, 1931.
4   GAMIO, Manuel. *Mexican Immigration to the United States: A Study of Human Migration and Adjustment*. Chicago, 1930.
5   GILMORE, N. Ray and Gladys W. "The Bracero in California." *Pac Hist Rev*, XXXII (1963), 265–282.
6   LEWIS, Oscar. *La Vida: A Puerto Rican Family in the Culture of Poverty—San Juan and New York*. New York, 1966.†
7   Mc WILLIAMS, Carey. *North from Mexico, The Spanish-Speaking People of the United States*. Philadelphia, 1949.
8   MOORE, Joan W. *Mexican-Americans: Problems and Prospects*. Los Angeles, 1967.
9   PITT, Leonard. *The Decline of the Californios: A Social History of the Spanish-Speaking Californians, 1846–1890*. Berkeley, 1966.
10 ROBINSON, Cecil. "Spring Water with a Taste of the Land: The Mexican Presence in the American Southwest." *Am W*, III (1966), 6–15, 95.
11 SERVIN, Manuel P. "The Pre-World War II Mexican-American: An Interpretation." *Cal Hist Soc Q*, XLV (1966), 325–338.
12 SEXTON, Patricia C. *Spanish Harlem: Anatomy of Poverty*. New York, 1965.†
13 WALTERS, Thorstina. *Modern Sagas: The Story of the Icelanders in North America*. Fargo, N.D., 1953.

E. Negroes

1. GENERAL

14 BALDWIN, James. *The Fire Next Time*. New York, 1963.†
15 BALDWIN, James. *Notes of a Native Son*. Boston, 1968.†
16 BLAIR, Lewis A. *A Southern Prophecy: The Prosperity of the South Dependent upon the Elevation of the Negro*. Boston, 1889; 1964.
17 BROWN, Claude. *Manchild in the Promised Land*. New York, 1965.
18 CLARK, Kenneth Bancroft, and Talcott PARSONS, eds. *The Negro American*. Boston, 1966.

1 DAVID, Jay. *Growing Up Black.* New York, 1968.
2 DAVIS, Allison, and John DOLLARD. *Children of Bondage.* New York, 1940.
3 DONALD, H. H. *The Negro Freedman.* New York, 1952.
4 DRAKE, St. Clair, and H. R. CAYTON. *Black Metropolis.* New York, 1945.
5 DU BOIS, W. E. B. *The Philadelphia Negro: A Social Study.* New York, 1899; 1967.†
6 DU BOIS, W. E. B., ed. *The Negro American Family.* Cambridge, Mass., 1970.†
7 ELLISON, Ralph. *The Invisible Man.* New York, 1952.
8 FARLEY, Reynolds. "The Urbanization of Negroes in The United States." *J Soc Hist,* I (1966-68), 241-258.
9 FISHEL, Leslie H. Jr., and Benjamin QUARLES. *The Negro American: A Documentary History.* Chicago, 1967.†
10 FRANKLIN, John Hope. *From Slavery to Freedom: A History of American Negroes.* New York, 1956.†
11 FRAZIER, E. Franklin. *Black Bourgeoisie.* New York, 1957.†
12 FRAZIER, E. Franklin. *The Free Negro Family.* New York, 1968.
13 FRAZIER, E. Franklin. *The Negro Family in the United States.* Chicago, 1966.†
14 FRAZIER, E. Franklin. *The Negro in the United States.* New York, 1957.
15 GLENN, Norval D. "Some Changes in the Relative Status of American Nonwhites, 1940 to 1969." *Phylon* XXIV (1963), 109-122.
16 GOLDSTON, Robert C. *The Negro Revolution.* New York, 1968.
17 GORDON, Milton M. *Assimilation in American Life: The Role of Race, Religion, and National Origins.* New York, 1964.†
18 GRIER, William H., and Price M. COBBS. *Black Rage.* New York, 1968.
19 HANDLIN, Oscar. *The Newcomers: Negroes and Puerto Ricans in a Changing Metropolis.* Cambridge, Mass., 1959.†
20 HIGGINSON, Thomas Wentworth. *Army Life in a Black Regiment.* See 4.15.
21 HILL, Herbert, ed. *Anger and Beyond: The Negro Writer in the United States.* New York, 1968.
22 ISAACS, Harold R. *The New World of Negro Americans.* New York, 1963.†
23 JOHNSON, Charles S. *Growing up in the Black Belt: Negro Youth in the Rural South.* New York, 1967.
24 LOGAN, Rayford W. *The Negro in American Life and Thought: The Nadir, 1877-1901.* New York, 1954.
25 MILLER, Elizabeth W., ed. *The Negro in America: A Bibliography.* See 2.14.

1. MYRDAL, Gunnar. *An American Dilemma: The Negro Problem and Modern Democracy.* New York, 1944.

2. OSOFSKY, Gilbert. *Harlem: The Making of a Ghetto. Negro New York, 1890–1930.* New York, 1966.†

3. OVINGTON, Mary White. *Half a Man, The Status of the Negro in New York.* New York, 1911.

4. PEASE, William H. and Jane H. *Black Uptopia: Negro Communal Experiments in America.* Madison, Wis., 1963.

5. QUINT, Howard H. *Profile in Black and White: A Frank Portrait of South Carolina.* See 13.12.

6. RAINWATER, Lee, and William L. YANCEY. *The Moynihan Report and the Politics of Controversy.* Cambridge, Mass., 1967.†

7. RECORD, Wilson. *The Negro and the Communist Party.* Chapel Hill, 1951.

8. RECORD, Wilson. *Race and Radicalism: The NAACP and the Communist Party in Conflict.* Ithaca, N.Y., 1964.†

9. ROSE, Arnold M. ed. "The Negro Protest," *Ann Am Acad Pol Soc Sci,* CCCLVII (Jan. 1965), ix–133.

10. SMITH Timothy Lynn. "The Redistribution of the Negro Population of the United States, 1910–1960." See 22.5.

11. SPEAR, Allan H. *Black Chicago: The Making of a Negro Ghetto, 1890–1920.* Chicago, 1967.

12. TAEUBER, Karl E. and Alma F. *Negroes in Cities: Residential Segregation and Neighborhood Change.* Chicago, 1965.

13. U.S. National Advisory Commission on Civil Disorders. *Report.* Washington, D.C., 1969.†

14. WARREN, Robert Penn. *Who Speaks for the Negro?* New York, 1965.†

15. WELSCH, Erwin K. *The Negro in the United States: A Research Guide.* Bloomington, Ind., 1964.

16. WRIGHT, Richard. *Native Son.* Chicago, 1940.

2. NEGRO HISTORY

17. DRIMMER, Melvin, ed. *Black History: A Reappraisal.* New York, 1968.

18. FRANKLIN, John Hope. "The Two Worlds of Race: A Historical View." *Daedalus,* XCIV (1965), 899–920.

19. FRANKLIN, John Hope. "The New Negro History," *J Neg Hist,* XLII (1957), 89–97.

20. GRANT, Joanne, ed. *Black Protest: History, Documents, and Analyses, 1619 to the Present.* New York, 1968.

21. GREEN, Constance McLaughlin. *The Secret City: A History of Race Relations in the Nation's Capital.* Princeton, 1967.

22. HIRSHSON, Stanley P. *Farewell to the Bloody Shirt: Northern Republicans and the Southern Negro, 1877–1893.* Chicago, 1968.†

1. HUGHES, Langston. *Fight for Freedom: The Story of the NAACP.* New York, 1962.
2. HUGHES, Langston, and Milton MELTZER. *A Pictorial History of the Negro in America.* New York, 1963.
3. KATZ, William L., ed. *Eyewitness: The Negro in American History.* New York, 1967.†
4. KELLOGG, Charles Flint. *NAACP: A History of the National Association for the Advancement of Colored People.* Baltimore, 1967.
5. LOGAN, Frenise A. *The Negro in North Carolina, 1876–1894.* Chapel Hill, 1964.†
6. LOGAN, Rayford W. *The Negro in the United States.* Princeton, 1957.
7. McPHERSON, James M. *Marching Toward Freedom: The Negro in the Civil War, 1861–1865.* New York, 1968.
8. McPHERSON, James M. *The Struggle for Equality: Abolitionists and the Negro in the Civil War and Reconstruction.* Princeton, 1964.†
9. MEIER, August, and Elliott M. RUDWICK. *From Plantation to Ghetto: An Interpretive History of American Negroes.* New York, 1966.†
10. MILLER, Elizabeth W., comp. *The Negro in America: A Bibliography.* See 2.14.
11. MUSE, Benjamin. *The American Negro Revolution: From Non-Violence to Black Power, 1963–1967.* Bloomington, 1968.
12. OTTLEY, Roi, and William J. WEATHERBY, eds. *The Negro in New York. An Informal Social History.* New York, 1967.
13. REDDING, Saunders. *The Lonesome Road: The Story of the Negro's Part in America.* New York, 1958.†
14. ROSE, Arnold M. *The Negro in America.* New York, 1948.†
15. ROSE, Willie Lee. *Rehearsal for Reconstruction: The Port Royal Experiment.* Indianapolis, 1964.
16. SCHEINER, Seth M. *Negro Mecca: A History of the Negro in New York City, 1865–1920.* New York, 1965.
17. STERNSHER, Bernard, ed. *The Negro in Depression and War.* Chicago, 1969.
18. THORPE, Earl E. *Negro Historians in the United States.* Baton Rouge 1958.
19. THORPE, Earl E. *The Mind of the Negro: An Intellectual History of Afro-Americans.* Baton Rouge, 1961.
20. TINDALL, George Brown. *South Carolina Negroes, 1877–1900.* Columbia, S.C., 1952.†
21. WILEY, Bell Irvin. *Southern Negroes, 1861–1865.* New Haven, 1965.†
22. WILLIAMSON, Joel. *After Slavery: The Negro in South Carolina During Reconstruction, 1861–1877.* Chapel Hill, 1965.†
23. WRIGHT, Richard, and Edwin ROSSKAM. *12 Million Black Voices,* New York, 1941.

1 WYNES, Charles E., ed. *The Negro in the South Since 1865: Selected Essays in American Negro History.* Tuscaloosa, Ala., 1965.

3. RACE RELATIONS AND RACIAL PROTEST

2 BENNETT, Lerone, Jr. *Confrontation: Black and White.* Chicago, 1965.

3 BENNETT, Lerone, Jr. *Black Power, U.S.A.: The Human Side of Reconstruction, 1867–1877.* Chicago, 1967.

4 BRINK, William, and Louis HARRIS. *The Negro Revolution in America.* New York, 1964.

5 BURNS, W. Haywood. *The Voices of Negro Protest in America.* New York, 1963.

6 CABLE, George Washington. *The Negro Question: A Selection of Writings on Civil Rights in the South.* New York, 1958.

7 CARMICHAEL, Stokely, and Charles V. HAMILTON. *Black Power. The Politics of Liberation in America.* New York, 1967.†

8 COLES, Robert. *Children of Crisis: A Study of Courage and Fear.* New York, 1967.†

9 DULLES, Foster Rhea. *The Civil Rights Commission: 1957–1965.* Lansing, Mich., 1968.

10 ESSIEN-UDOM, E. U. *Black Nationalism: A Search for an Identity in America.* New York, 1962.†

11 FRANKLIN, John Hope, and Isidore STARR. *The Negro in Twentieth Century America: A Reader on the Struggle for Civil Rights.* New York, 1967.†

12 FURNAS, Joseph C. *Goodbye to Uncle Tom.* New York, 1956.†

13 KING, Martin Luther. *Stride Toward Freedom: The Montgomery Story.* New York, 1958.†

14 LINCOLN, C. Eric. *The Black Muslims in America.* Boston, 1961.†

15 LOMAX, Louis E. *The Negro Revolt.* New York, 1962.†

16 NEWBY, I. A. *Jim Crow's Defense: Anti-Negro Thought in America, 1900–1930.* Baton Rouge, 1965.†

17 NOLEN, Claude H. *The Negro's Image in the South: The Anatomy of White Supremacy.* Lexington, Ky., 1967.†

18 OSOFSKY, Gilbert, ed. *The Burden of Race. A Documentary History of Negro-White Relations in America.* New York, 1967.†

19 RUDWICK, Elliott M. *Race Riot at East St. Louis, July 2, 1917.* Carbondale, Ill., 1964.†

20 SEABROOK, Isaac D. *Before and After: Or the Relations of the Races at the South.* Ed. by John Hammond Moore. See 5.3.

21 SHOGAN, Robert, and Tom CRAIG. *The Detroit Race Riot: A Study in Violence.* Philadelphia, 1964.

22 SILVER, James W. *Mississippi: The Closed Society.* New York, 1964.†

1 THORNBROUGH, Emma Lou. *The Negro in Indiana: A Study of a Minority.* Indianapolis, 1957.
2 WASKOW, Arthur I. *From Race Riot to Sit-In, 1919 and the 1960's: A Study in the Connections Between Conflict and Violence.* Garden City, N.Y., 1966.†
3 WOOD, Forrest G. *Black Scare: The Racist Response to Emancipation and Reconstruction.* Berkeley, 1967.
4 WOODWARD, C. Vann. *The Strange Career of Jim Crow.* New York, 1966.†
5 WYNES, Charles E. *Race Relations in Virginia, 1870–1902.* Charlottesville, Va., 1961.
6 ZINN, Howard. *SNCC: The New Abolitionists.* Boston, 1965.†

4. CULTURE, EDUCATION, AND RELIGION

7 BOND, Horace M. *The Education of the Negro in the American Social Order.* Rev. ed. New York, 1966.
8 BOND, Horace M. *Negro Education in Alabama: A Study in Cotton and Steel.* New York, 1966.†
9 BONE, Robert A. *The Negro Novel in America.* New Haven, 1965.
10 BULLOCK, Henry A. *A History of Negro Education in the South: From 1619 to the Present.* Cambridge, Mass., 1967.
11 CRIPPS, Thomas R. "The Death of Rastus: Negroes in American Films Since 1945." *Phylon* XXVIII (1967), 267–275.
12 DU BOIS, W. E. B. *The Negro Church.* Atlanta, Ga., 1903.
13 FRAZIER, E. Franklin. *The Negro Church in America.* New York, 1963.†
14 HARLAN, Louis R. *Separate and Unequal: Public School Campaigns and Racism in Southern Seaboard States 1901–1915.* New York, 1968.†
15 HERNDON, James. *The Way It Spozed to Be.* New York, 1968.†
16 "Higher Education of Negro Americans. Prospects and Programs." *J Neg Educ,* XXXVI (1967), 187–347.
17 LOCKE, Alain. *The New Negro: An Interpretation.* N.Y., 1968.
18 MEIER, August. *Negro Thought in America, 1880–1915: Racial Ideologies in the Age of Booker T. Washington.* Ann Arbor, Mich., 1963.
19 MILLER, Robert Moats. "Attitudes of American Protestantism toward the Negro, 1919–1939." *J Neg Hist,* XLI (1956), 215–240.
20 OSOFSKY, Gilbert. "Symbols of the Jazz Age: The New Negro and Harlem Discovered." *Am Q,* XVII (1965), 229–238.
21 RUBIN, Louis D., Jr., ed. *Teach the Freeman: The Correspondence of Rutherford B. Hayes and the Slater Fund for Negro Education.* 2 vols. Baton Rouge, 1959.
22 SWINT, Henry L., ed. *Dear Ones at Home: Letters from Contraband Camps.* Nashville, Tenn., 1966.

1. SWINT, Henry L. *The Northern Teacher in the South, 1862–1870.* New York, 1967.
2. WASHINGTON, Joseph R. *Black Religion: The Negro and Christianity in the United States.* Boston, 1964.†
3. WEATHERFORD, W. D. *American Churches and the Negro.* North Quincy, Mass. 1957.
4. WEST, Earl H. "The Peabody Education Fund and Negro Education, 1867–1880." *Hist Ed Q*, VI (1966), 3–21.
5. WISH, Harvey. "Negro Education and the Progressive Movement." *J Neg Hist*, XLIX (1964), 184–200.

5. EMPLOYMENT

6. BLOCH, Herman D. "Craft Unions and the Negro in History." *J Neg Hist.*, XLIII (1958), 10–33.
7. BLOCH Herman D. "Labor and the Negro 1866–1910," *J Neg Hist*, L(1965), 163–184.
8. HAYNES, George E. *The Negro at Work in New York City.* New York, 1968.†
9. JACOBSON, Julius, ed., *The Negro and the American Labor Movement.* Garden City, N.Y. 1968.†
10. KRISLOV, Samuel. *The Negro in Federal Employment: The Quest for Equal Opportunity.* Minneapolis, 1967.
11. MARSHALL, F. Ray. *The Negro Worker.* New York, 1967.
12. RUCHAMES, Louis. *Race, Jobs, and Politics: The Story of FEPC.* New York, 1953.
13. WESLEY, Charles H. *Negro Labor in the United States, 1850–1925: A Study in American Economic History.* New York, 1927.

6. LEADERSHIP

14. BARDOLPH, Richard. *The Negro Vanguard.* New York, 1959.†
15. BENNETT, Lerone, Jr. *What Manner of Man: A Biography of Martin Luther King, Jr.* New York, 1964.†
16. BRODERICK, Francis L. *W. E. B. Du Bois: Negro Leader in a Time of Crisis.* Stanford, Calif., 1959.†
17. CALISTA, Donald J. "Booker T. Washington: Another Look." *J Neg Hist.* XLIX (1964), 240–255.
18. CARPENTER, John A. *Sword and Olive Branch: Oliver Otis Howard.* Pittsburgh, 1964.
19. COULTER, E. Merton. *Negro Legislators in Georgia During the Reconstruction Period.* Athens, Ga., 1968.
20. CRONON, Edmund David. *Black Moses: The Story of Marcus Garvey and the Universal Negro Improvement Association.* Madison, Wis., 1955.†
21. DOUGLASS, Frederick. *Life and Times of Frederick Douglass: The Complete Autobiography.* N.Y., 1881; 1966.

1. DU BOIS, William E. B. *The Autobiography of W. E. B. Du Bois: A Soliloquy on Viewing My Life from the Last Decade of Its First Century.* New York, 1968.†
2. GRAHAM, Shirley. *There Once Was a Slave: The Heroic Story of Frederick Douglass.* New York, 1947.
3. HARLAN, Louis R. "Booker T. Washington and the White Man's Burden." *Am Hist Rev* LXXI (1966), 441–467.
4. HOLT, Rackham. *Mary McLeod Bethune: A Biography.* New York, 1964.
5. HUGHES, William H., and Frederick D. PATTERSON, eds. *Robert Russa Moton of Hampton and Tuskegee.* Chapel Hill, 1956.
6. MALCOLM X, and Alex HALEY. *The Autobiography of Malcolm X.* New York, 1966.†
7. MATHEWS, Basil. *Booker T. Washington, Educator and Interracial Interpreter.* Cambridge, Mass., 1948.
8. PUTTKAMMER, Charles W., and Ruth WORTHY. "William Monroe Trotter, 1872–1934." *J Neg Hist*, XLIII (1958), 298–316.
9. QUARLES, Benjamin, comp. *Frederick Douglass.* New York, 1968.†
10. RUDWICK, Elliott M. *W. E. B. Du Bois: A Study in Minority Group Leadership.* Philadelphia, 1961.
11. SPENCER, Samuel R., Jr. *Booker T. Washington and the Negro's Place in American Life.* New York, 1955.†
12. WASHINGTON, Booker T. *Up From Slavery, An Autobiography.* New York, 1901.†
13. WEBB, Constance. *Richard Wright: A Biography.* New York, 1968.

F. Indians

14. ADAMS, Evelyn C. *American Indian Education: Government Schools and Economic Progress.* New York, 1946.
15. BEAVER, R. Pierce. *Church, State, and the American Indians: Two and a Half Centuries of Partnership between Protestant Churches and Government.* St. Louis, Mo., 1966.
16. BERRY, Brewton. *Almost White.* New York, 1963.
17. BROPHY, William A. et al., comps. *The Indian: America's Unfinished Business. Report of the Commission on the Rights, Liberties, and Responsibilities of the American Indian.* Norman, Okla., 1966.
18. DRIVER, Harold E. *Indians of North America.* Chicago, 1961.†
19. EWERS, John C. *Indian Life on the Upper Missouri.* Norman, Okla., 1968.
20. FRITZ, Henry E. *The Movement for Indian Assimilation, 1860–1890.* Philadelphia, 1963.
21. GRINNELL, George B. *Pawnee, Blackfoot and Cheyenne: History and Folklore of the Plains.* New York, 1961.

1 HAGAN, William T. *American Indians.* Chicago, 1961.
2 HODGE, Frederick Webb. *Handbook of American Indians North of Mexico.* 2 vols., New York, 1968.
3 KELLY, Lawrence C. *The Navajo Indians and Federal Indian Policy, 1900-1935.* Tucson, Ariz., 1968.
4 MERIAM, Lewis. *The Problem of Indian Administration.* Washington, D.C., 1928.
5 MEYER, Roy W. *History of the Santee Sioux: United States Indian Policy on Trial.* Lincoln, Neb., 1968.
6 OEHLER, Chester M. *The Great Sioux Uprising.* New York, 1959.
7 PRATT, Richard Henry. *Battlefield and Classroom: Four Decades with the American Indian, 1867-1904.* New Haven, 1964.
8 SANDOZ, Mari. *Crazy Horse: The Strange Man of The Oglalas.* Lincoln, Neb., 1961.†
9 SIMPSON, George E., and J. Milton YINGER, eds. "American Indians and American Life." *Ann Am Acad Pol Soc Sci,* CCCXI (May 1957), vii-165.
10 U.S. Department of the Interior. *Soldier and Brave: Indian and Military Affairs in the Trans-Mississippi West, Including a Guide to Historical Sites and Landmarks.* Washington, D.C., 1963.
11 VESTAL, Stanley. *Sitting Bull, Champion of the Sioux: A Biography.* Norman, Okla., 1965.
12 WASHBURN, Wilcomb E., ed. *The Indian and the White Man.* New York, 1964.†
13 WELTFISH, Gene. *The Lost Universe.* New York, 1965.

G. Women

14 ANDERSON, Mary. *Woman at Work: The Autobiography of Mary Anderson as Told to Mary N. Winslow.* Minneapolis, Minn., 1951.
15 ANTHONY, Katherine. *Susan B. Anthony: Her Personal History and Her Era.* Garden City, N.Y., 1954.
16 BAKER, Elizabeth F. *Technology and Women's Work.* New York, 1964.
17 BLUMBERG, Dorothy Rose. *Florence Kelley: The Making of a Social Pioneer.* New York, 1966.
18 BRADWAY, John S., ed. "Progress in Family Law," *Ann Am Acad Pol Soc Sci,* CCCLXXXIII (May, 1969), ix-144.
19 BRECKINRIDGE, Sophonisba P. *Women in The Twentieth Century. A Study of Their Political, Social and Economic Activities.* New York, 1933.
20 BROWN, Dee. *The Gentle Tamers: Women in the Old Wild West.* See 13.22.
21 DAVIS, Allen F. "The Women's Trade Union League: Origins and Organization." *Lab Hist,* V (1964), 5-17.

1 DEGLER, Carl N. "Charlotte Perkins Gilman on the Theory and Practice of Feminism." *Am Q*, VIII (1956), 21–39.

2 EARHART, Mary. *Frances Willard: From Prayers to Politics.* Chicago, 1944.

3 FLEXNER, Eleanor. *Century of Struggle; The Women's Rights Movement in the United States.* Cambridge, Mass., 1959.†

4 GOLDMARK, Josephine. *Impatient Crusader: Florence Kelley's Life Story.* Urbana, Ill., 1953.

5 GRIMES, Alan P. *The Puritan Ethic and Woman Suffrage.* New York, 1967.

6 GROVES, Ernest R. *The American Woman; The Feminine Side of a Masculine Civilization.* Rev. ed. New York, 1944.

7 GRUENBERG, Sidonie M., and H. S. KRECH. *Many Lives of Modern Woman.* Garden City, N.Y., 1952.

8 HAYS, Elinor R. *Morning Star: A Biography of Lucy Stone, 1818–1893.* New York, 1961.

9 KRADITOR, Aileen S. *The Ideas of the Woman Suffrage Movement, 1890–1920.* New York, 1965.

10 LIFTON, Robert Jay, ed. *The Woman in America.* Boston, 1966.†

11 LUTZ, Alma. *Susan B. Anthony: Rebel, Crusader, Humanitarian.* Boston, 1959.

12 Mc GOVERN, James R. "The American Woman's Pre-World War I Freedom in Manners and Morals." *J Am Hist* LV (1968), 315–333.

13 MARKS, Jeannette. *Life and Letters of Mary Emma Woolley.* Washington, D.C., 1955.

14 MASSEY, Mary Elizabeth. *Bonnet Brigades.* See 4.17.

15 MEAD, Margaret, and Frances B. KAPLAN, eds. *American Women: The Report of the President's Commission on the Status of Women, and Other Publications of the Commission.* New York, 1966.†

16 NEWCOMER, Mabel. *A Century of Higher Education for American Women.* New York, 1959.

17 PECK, Mary Gray. *Carrie Chapman Catt.* New York, 1944.

18 POTTER, David M. "American Women and the American Character." *Stetson Univ Bull*, LXII, (1962), 1–22.

19 RIEGEL, Robert E. *American Feminists.* Lawrence, Kan., 1963.

20 ROGERS, Agnes. *Women are Here to Stay.* New York, 1949.

21 SCOTT, Anne Firor. "After Suffrage: Southern Women in the Twenties." *J S Hist*, XXX (1964), 298–318.

22 SINCLAIR, Andrew. *The Better Half.* New York, 1965.

23 SINCLAIR, Andrew. *The Emancipation of the American Woman.* New York, 1966.

1 SMUTS, Robert W. *Women and Work in America.* New York, 1959.
2 SOLLID, Roberta Beed. *Calamity Jane: A Study in Historical Criticism.* Helena, Mont., 1958.
3 STERN, Madeleine B. *We the Women: Career Firsts of Nineteenth-Century America.* New York, 1963.
4 STRAYER, Martha. *The D. A. R.: An Informal History.* Washington, D.C., 1958.
5 WILLARD, Frances Elizabeth. *Glimpses of Fifty Years; The Autobiography of an American Woman.* Chicago, 1889.
6 WILLARD, Frances Elizabeth, and Mary A. LIVERMORE. *Portraits and Biographies of Prominent American Women.* New York, 1901.
7 WOODY, Thomas. *A History of Women's Education in the United States.* 2 vols. New York, 1929; 1966.

H. The Family

8 ANSHEN, Ruth Nanda, ed. *The Family.* New York, 1959.
9 BLAKE, Nelson M. *The Road to Reno: The History of Divorce in the United States.* New York, 1962.
10 BUSBEY, Katherine. *Home Life in America.* New York, 1910.
11 CALHOUN, Arthur W. *A Social History of the American Family.* 3 vols. Cleveland, 1919.
12 CLARKE, Helen I. *Social Legislation: American Laws Dealing with the Family, Child, and Dependent.* New York, 1940.
13 DITZION, Sidney. *Marriage, Morals, and Sex in America: A History of Ideas.* New York, 1953.
14 DU BOIS, W. E. B., ed. *The Negro American Family.* See 27.6.
15 GLICK, Paul C. *American Families*, New York, 1957.
16 GOLDSTEIN, Joseph, and Jay KATZ. *The Family and the Law.* New York, 1965.
17 GROVES, Ernest R. *The Contemporary American Family.* Philadelphia, 1947.
18 HARPER, Fowler V. *Problems of the Family.* Indianapolis, 1952. Rev. ed. 1962.
19 HILL, Reuben. *Families Under Stress.* New York, 1949.
20 JACOBSON, Paul. *American Marriage and Divorce.* New York, 1959.
21 KINSEY, A. C. et al. *Sexual Behavior in the Human Female.* Philadelphia, 1953.
22 KINSEY, A. C. et al. *Sexual Behavior in the Human Male.* Philadelphia, 1948.
23 O'NEILL, William L. *Divorce in the Progressive Era.* New Haven, 1967.

1 RAINWATER, Lee. *And the Poor Get Children: Sex, Contraception, and Family Planning in the Working Class.* Chicago, 1960.

2 SAVETH, Edward N., ed. "The Problem of American Family History," *Am Q*, XXI (Summer 1969), 311–329.

3 SCHLESINGER, Arthur M. *Learning How to Behave.* New York, 1946; 1968.

4 SIRJAMAKI, John. *The American Family in the Twentieth Century.* Cambridge, Mass., 1953.

5 STOUFFER, Samuel Andrew et al. *Research Memorandum on the Family in The Depression.* New York, 1937.

6 STRECKER, Edward Adam. *Their Mothers' Sons; The Psychiatrist Examines an American Problem.* Philadelphia, 1951.

7 WYLIE, Philip. *Generation of Vipers.* New York, 1942.†

8 YOUNG, Kimball. *Isn't One Wife Enough?* New York, 1954.

J. Children and Youth

9 ABBOTT, Grace. *The Child and the State.* 2 vols. Chicago, 1938.

10 BELL, Howard M. *Youth Tell Their Story: A Study of the Conditions and Attitudes of Young People.* Washington, D.C., 1938.

11 BELL, Winifred. *Aid to Dependent Children.* New York, 1965.

12 BERNARD, Jessie, ed. "Teen Age Culture", *Ann Am Acad Pol Soc Sci*, CCCXXXVIII (Nov. 1961), vii–136.

13 BOURNE, Randolph. *Youth and Life.* New York, 1913; 1967.

14 BRACE, Charles Loring. *The Dangerous Classes of New York and Twenty Years' Work Among Them.* New York, 1872.

15 BURCHINAL, Lee G. *Rural Youth in Crisis: Facts, Myths, and Social Change.* Washington, D.C., 1964.

16 CICOUREL, Aaron V. *The Social Organization of Juvenile Justice.* New York, 1968.

17 COLES, Robert. *Children of Crisis.* See 30.8.

18 COMSTOCK, Anthony. *Traps for the Young.* Cambridge, Mass., 1967.

19 DAVIS, Allison, and John DOLLARD. *Children of Bondage.* See 27.2.

20 EDDY, Sherwood. *A Century with Youth: A History of the Y.M.C.A. from 1844 to 1944.* New York, 1944.

21 ERIKSON, Erik H., ed. *Youth: Change and Challenge.* New York, 1963.†

22 FELT, Jeremy P. *Hostages of Fortune: Child Labor Reform in New York State.* Syracuse, 1965.

23 FOLKS, Homer. *The Care of Destitute, Neglected, and Delinquent Children.* New York, 1902.

24 HOLLINGSHED, August B. *Elmtown's Youth.* New York, 1949.†

1. HOPKINS, Charles H. *A History of the Y.M.C.A. in North America.* New York, 1951.
2. KADUSHIN, Alfred. *Child Welfare Services.* New York, 1967.
3. KEITH-LUCAS, Alan, ed. "Programs and Problems in Child Welfare." *Ann Am Acad Pol Soc Sci,* CCCLV (Sept. 1964), 1–129.
4. LANGSAM, Miriam Z. *Children West: A History of the Placing-Out System of the New York Children's Aid Society, 1853–1890.* Madison, Wis., 1964.
5. LINDLEY, Betty and Ernest K. *A New Deal for Youth.* New York, 1938.
6. LORWIN, Lewis L. *Youth Work Programs.* Washington, D.C., 1941.
7. LUMPKIN, Katherine, and Dorothy DOUGLAS. *Child Workers in America.* New York, 1937.
8. LUNDBERG, Emma Octavia. *Unto the Least of These: Social Services for Children.* New York, 1947.
9. MANGOLD, George B. *Problems of Child Welfare.* New York, 1914.
10. MEAD, Margaret, and M. WOLFENSTEIN, eds. *Childhood in Contemporary Culture.* Chicago, 1955.
11. MINEHAN, Thomas. *Boy and Girl Tramps in America.* New York, 1934.
12. SPARGO, John. *The Bitter Cry of the Children.* New York, 1906.†
13. THURSTON, Henry W. *The Dependent Child.* New York, 1930.
14. TRATTNER, Walter I. *Crusade for the Children.* Chicago, 1970.
15. TRATTNER, Walter I. *Homer Folks, Pioneer in Social Welfare.* New York, 1968.
16. WHYTE, William F. *Street Corner Society, The Social Structure of an Italian Slum.* See 20.7.
17. WOLFE, Tom. *The Pump House Gang.* See 22.1.
18. WOOD, Stephen B. *Constitutional Politics in the Progressive Era: Child Labor and the Law.* Chicago, 1968.

VI. The American and His Work

A. General

19. COWING, Cedric B. *Populists, Plungers and Progressives: A Social History of Stock and Commodity Speculation.* Princeton, 1965.†
20. DOUGLAS, Paul H. *Real Wages in the United States, 1890–1926.* New York, 1930.
21. FELS, Rendigs. *American Business Cycles, 1865–1897.* Chapel Hill, 1959.
22. FRIEDMAN, Milton, and Anna J. SCHWARTZ. *A Monetary History of the U.S., 1867–1960.* Princeton, 1964.

1 GALBRAITH, John Kenneth. *The Affluent Society.* New York, 1958.†
2 GALBRAITH, John Kenneth. *The Great Crash.* See 8.1.
3 GOODRICH, Carter. *Government Promotion of American Canals and Railroads: 1800–1890.* New York, 1960.
4 LIVELY, Robert A. "The American System: A Review Article" *Bus Hist Rev*, XXIX (March 1955) 81–96.
5 MAYO, Elton. *The Human Problems of an Industrial Civilization.* New York, 1933.
6 NORTH, Douglass C. *Growth and Welfare in the American Past: A New Economic History.* Englewood Cliffs, N.J., 1966.†
7 RATNER, Sidney. *American Taxation.* New York, 1942.†
8 SOULE, George. *Prosperity Decade.* See 8.24.
9 WOYTINSKY, Emma S. *Profile of the U.S. Economy: A Survey of Growth and Change.* New York, 1966.
10 YELLOWITZ, Irwin. *The Position of the Worker in American Society, 1865–1896.* Englewood Cliffs, N.J., 1969.

B. Technology

11 ANDERSON, Oscar E. Jr., *Refrigeration in America: A History of a New Technology and Its Impact.* Princeton, 1953.
12 BRIGHT, Arthur A. *The Electric-Lamp Industry: Technological Change and Economic Development from 1800 to 1947.* New York, 1949.
13 CHASE, Stuart. *Men and Machines.* New York, 1929.
14 CURRENT, Richard N. *The Typewriter and the Men Who Made It.* Urbana, Ill., 1954.
15 GIEDION, Siegfried. *Mechanization Takes Command: A Contribution to Anonymous History.* New York, 1948.
16 JOSEPHSON, Matthew. *Edison.* New York, 1959.†
17 KELLY, Fred C. *The Wright Brothers.* New York, 1943.†
18 MITCHELL, Broadus, and George S. MITCHELL. *The Industrial Revolution in the South.* Baltimore, 1930.
19 MORISON, Elting E. *Men, Machines, and Modern Times.* Cambridge, Mass., 1966.†
20 OLIVER, J. W. *History of American Technology.* New York, 1956.
21 ROLT, Lionel T. *A Short History of Machine Tools.* Cambridge, Mass., 1965.
22 SHARLIN, Harold T. *The Making of the Electrical Age: From the Telegraph to Automation.* New York, 1963.
23 STREET, James H. *The New Revolution in the Cotton Economy: Mechanization and Its Consequences.* Chapel Hill, 1957.
24 *Technology and the American Economy: Report of the National Commission on Technology, Automation, and Economic Progress.* Washington, D.C., 1966.

1 VAUGHAN, Floyd Lamar. *The United States Patent System*. Norman, Okla., 1956.

2 WIK, Reynold M. *Steam Power on The American Farm*. Philadelphia, 1953.

C. Agriculture

1. GENERAL

3 BAKER, Gladys L. et al. *Century of Service, the First 100 Years of the United States Department of Agriculture*. Washington, D.C., 1963.

4 BAKER, Olin Edwin, et al. *Agriculture in Modern Life*. New York, 1939.

5 BOGUE, Allan G. *From Prairie to Corn Belt: Farming on the Illinois and Iowa Prairies in the Nineteenth Century*. See 11.1.

6 BOGUE, Allan G. *Money at Interest: The Farm Mortage on the Middle Border*. Ithaca, N.Y., 1955.†

7 BOGUE, Margaret B. *Patterns from the Sod: Land Use and Tenure in the Grand Prairie, 1850–1900*. See 15.1.

8 CARSTENSEN, Vernon. *Farms or Forests: Evolution of a State Land Policy for Northern Wisconsin, 1850–1932*. Madison, Wis., 1958.

9 CONRAD, David Eugene. *The Forgotten Farmers: The Story of Sharecroppers in the New Deal*. Urbana, Ill., 1965.

10 DANA, Samuel T. *Forest and Range Policy: Its Development in the United States*. New York, 1956.

11 FITE, Gilbert C. *The Farmer's Frontier, 1865–1900*. New York, 1966.

12 GATES, Paul W. *Agriculture and the Civil War*. See 4.14.

13 HAYTER, Earl W. *The Troubled Farmer, 1850–1900: Rural Adjustment to Industrialism*. De Kalb, Ill., 1968.

14 HEADY, Earl O. et al. *Roots of the Farm Problem*. Ames, Iowa, 1965.

15 LAMPARD, Eric E. *The Rise of the Dairy Industry in Wisconsin: A Study in Agricultural Change*. Madison, Wis., 1963.

16 Mc WILLIAMS, Carey. *Ill Fares the Land: Migrants and Migratory Labor in the United States*. Boston, 1944.

17 MALIN, James C. *Winter Wheat in the Golden Belt of Kansas*. Lawrence, Kan., 1944.

18 RANGE, Willard. *A Century of Georgia Agriculture, 1850–1950*. Athens, Ga., 1954.

19 SHANNON, Fred A. *The Farmer's Last Frontier: Agriculture, 1860–1897*. New York, 1945.†

20 SITTERSON, J. Carlyle. *Sugar Country: The Cane Sugar Industry in the South, 1753–1950*. Lexington, Ky., 1953.

THE AMERICAN AND HIS WORK 41

1. U.S. Department of Agriculture. *Farmers in a Changing World.* Washington, D.C., 1940.
2. U.S. President's Committee on Migratory Labor. *Migratory Labor in American Agriculture.* Washington, D.C., 1951.
3. WILCOX, Walter W. *The Farmer in the Second World War.* Ames, Iowa, 1947.
4. WRIGHT, Dale. *They Harvest Despair: The Migrant Farm Worker.* Boston, 1965.

2. RURAL LIFE

5. ANDERSON, Wilbert L. *The Country Town; A Study of Rural Evolution.* New York, 1906.
6. BRITT, Albert. *An America That Was: What Life Was Like on an Illinois Farm Seventy Years Ago.* See 11.2.
7. FULLER, Wayne E. *RFD: The Changing Face of Rural America.* Bloomington, 1964.
8. HIGBEE, Edward. *Farms and Farmers in an Urban Age.* New York, 1963.†
9. NEELY, Wayne C. *The Agricultural Fair.* New York, 1935.
10. POE, Clarence Hamilton. *Farm Life, Problems and Opportunities.* Chicago, 1931.
11. SCHAFER, Joseph. *The Social History of American Agriculture.* New York, 1936.
12. SHANNON Fred A. "Culture and Agriculture in America." *Miss Val Hist Rev* XLI (1954), 3–20.
13. VIDICH, Arthur J., and Joseph BENSMAN. *Small Town in Mass Society: Class, Power, and Religion in a Rural Community.* Princeton, 1958.†

3. AGRARIAN DISCONTENT, AGRARIAN MOVEMENTS AND GOVERNMENT POLICY

14. BARNS, William D. "Oliver Hudson Kelley and the Genesis of the Grange: A Reappraisal." *Ag Hist*, XLI (1967), 229–242.
15. BUCK, Solon J. *The Agrarian Crusade; A Chronicle of the Farmer in Politics.* New Haven, 1920.
16. BUCK, Solon J. *The Granger Movement.* Lincoln, Nebr., 1913.†
17. CAMPBELL, Christiana M. *The Farm Bureau and the New Deal: A Study of the Making of National Farm Policy, 1933–40.* Urbana, Ill., 1962.
18. CERNY, George. "Cooperation in the Midwest in the Granger Era, 1869–1875." *Ag Hist*, XXXVII (1963), 187–205.
19. CHAMBERS, Clarke A. *California Farm Organizations: A Historical Study of the Grange, The Farm Bureau, and the Associated Farmers, 1929–1941.* Berkeley, 1952.

1 CRAMPTON, John A. *The National Farmers Union: Idealogy of a Pressure Group*. Lincoln, Nebr., 1965.

2 FITE, Gilbert C. *Farm to Factory: A History of the Consumer Cooperative Association*. Columbia, Mo., 1965.

3 FITE, Gilbert C. "Farmer Opinion and the Agricultural Adjustment Act, 1933." *Miss Val Hist Rev* XLVIII (1962), 656–673.

4 HOGLUND, A. William, "A Comment on the Farm Strikes of 1932 and 1962." *Ag Hist*, XXXIX (1965), 213–216.

5 KEENER, Orrin L. *Struggle for Equal Opportunity: Dirt Farmers and the American Country Life Association*. New York, 1961.

6 SALOUTOS, Theodore. *Farmer Movements in the South, 1865–1933*. Berkeley, 1960.†

7 SALOUTOS, Theodore. "The Grange in the South, 1870–1877." *J S Hist*, XIX (1953), 473–487.

8 SALOUTOS, Theodore, and John D. HICKS. *Agricultural Discontent in the Middle West, 1900–1939*. Madison, Wis., 1951.†

9 SCHLEBECKER, John T. "The Great Holding Action: The NFO Strike in September, 1962." *Ag Hist*, XXXIX (1965), 204–213.

10 SCOTT, Roy V. *The Agrarian Movement in Illinois, 1880–1896*. Urbana, Ill., 1962.

11 SHANNON, Fred A. *American Farmer's Movements*. New York, 1957.†

12 SHIDELER, J. H. *Farm Crisis, 1919–1923*. Berkeley, 1957.

13 SHOVER, John L. *Cornbelt Rebellion: The Farmers' Holiday Association*. Urbana, Ill., 1965.

14 SHOVER, John L. "Populism in the Nineteen-Thirties: The Battle for the AAA." *Ag Hist*, XXXIX (1965), 17–24.

15 SIMKINS, Francis B. *Pitchfork Ben Tillman*. Baton Rouge, 1944.†

16 TAYLOR, Carl C. *Farmers' Movement, 1620–1920*. New York, 1953.

17 U.S. Farm Security Administration. *Disadvantaged Classes in American Agriculture*. Social Research Report No. 8. Washington, D.C., 1938.

18 WOODWARD, C. Vann. *Tom Watson: Agrarian Rebel*. New York, 1938.†

4. RANCHING AND THE COWBOY

19 ADAMS, Andy. *The Log of a Cowboy*. Lincoln, Nebr., 1903.†

20 ADAMS, Ramon F. *The Old Time Cowhand*. New York, 1961.

21 ADAMS, Ramon F. *The Rampaging Herd: A Bibliography of Books and Pamphlets on Men and Events in the Cattle Industry*. See 1.3.

22 ATHERTON, Lewis. *The Cattle Kings*. Bloomington, 1961.

23 DYKSTRA, Robert R. *The Cattle Towns*. See 14.4.

24 FRANTZ, Joe B., and Julian E. CHOATE, Jr. *The American Cowboy: The Myth and the Reality*. New York, 1955.

1 FRINK, Maurice et al. *When Grass Was King: Contributions to the Western Range Cattle Industry Study.* Boulder, Col., 1956.

2 GARD, Wayne. *The Chisholm Trail.* Norman, Okla., 1954.

3 Mc CALLUM, Henry D. and Frances T. *The Wire That Fenced the West.* Norman, Okla., 1965.

4 MALIN, James C. *The Grasslands of North America.* See 15.15.

5 SANDOZ, Mari. *The Buffalo Hunters: The Story of the Hide Men.* New York, 1954.

6 SCHLEBECKER, J. T. *Cattle Raising on the Plains, 1900–1961.* Lincoln, Neb., 1963.

D. Business, Commerce, and Industry

7 ALLEN, Frederick Lewis. *The Great Pierpont Morgan*, New York, 1949.†

8 BRIDGES, Hal. "The Robber Baron Concept in American History." *Bus Hist Rev*, XXXII (1958), 1–13.

9 BUDER, Stanley. *Pullman: An Experiment in Industrial Order and Community Planning, 1880–1930.* See 17.12.

10 CHANDLER, Alfred D., Jr. *Henry Varnum Poor: Business Editor, Analyst, and Reformer.* Cambridge, Mass., 1956.

11 CHEIT, Earl F., ed. *The Business Establishment.* New York, 1967.†

12 CLEMEN, R. A. *The American Livestock and Meat Industry.* New York, 1923.

13 COCHRAN, Thomas C. *The American Business System, 1900–1955.* New York, 1956.†

14 COCHRAN, Thomas C. "The History of a Business Society." *J Am Hist*, LIV (1967), 5–18.

15 COCHRAN, Thomas C., and W. MILLER. *The Age of Enterprise, A Social History of Industrial America.* New York, 1961.†

16 COWING, Cedric B. *Populists, Plungers, and Progressives: A Social History of Stock and Commodity Speculation, 1890–1936.* See 38.18.

17 DIAMOND, Sigmund. *The Reputation of the American Businessman.* New York, 1955.

18 FUCHS, Victor R. *Changes in the Location of Manufacturing in the United States since 1929.* New Haven, 1962.

19 HABER, Samuel. *Efficiency and Uplift: Scientific Management in the Progressive Era, 1890–1920.* Chicago, 1964.

20 HACKER, Louis M. *The World of Andrew Carnegie: 1865–1901.* Philadelphia, 1968.

21 HACKER, Louis M. *Triumph of American Capitalism.* New York, 1940.†

1. HAYS, Samuel P. *The Response to Industrialism, 1885–1914.* See 5.18.
2. HOLBROOK, Stewart H. *The Age of the Moguls.* New York, 1953.†
3. JENKINS, J. W. *James B. Duke: Master Builder.* New York, 1927.
4. JOSEPHSON, Matthew. *The Robber Barons,* New York, 1934.†
5. KIRKLAND, Edward C. *Dream and Thought in the Business Community, 1860–1900.* Chicago, 1956.†
6. KIRKLAND, Edward C. *Industry Comes of Age: Business, Labor, and Public Policy, 1860–1897.* Chicago, 1961.†
7. KOLKO, Gabriel. *Railroads and Regulation.* Princeton, 1965.
8. LARSON, Henrietta M. *Guide to Business History.* Cambridge, Mass., 1948.
9. LARSON, Henrietta M. *Jay Cooke, Private Banker.* Cambridge, Mass., 1936.
10. Mc DONALD, Forest. *Insull.* Chicago, 1962.
11. Mc DONALD, Forrest. *Let there Be Light: The Electric Utility Industry in Wisconsin, 1881–1955.* Chicago, 1957.
12. MILLER, William. "American Historians and the Business Elite." *J Econ Hist,* IX (1949), 184–208.
13. MILLER, William, ed. *Men in Business: Essays in the History of Entrepreneurship.* New York, 1952.†
14. NEVINS, Allan. *Study in Power: John D. Rockefeller, Industrialist and Philanthropist.* New York, 1953.
15. NEWCOMER, Mabel. *The Big Business Executive: The Factors that Made Him, 1900–1950.* New York, 1955.
16. PRESBREY, Frank S. *The History and Development of Advertising.* New York, 1929.
17. PROTHRO, James W. *The Dollar Decade; Business Ideas in the 1920s.* Baton Rouge, 1954.
18. SUTTON, Francis X. et al. *The American Business Creed.* Cambridge, Mass., 1956.†
19. TARBELL, Ida M. *The Nationalizing of Business, 1878–1898.* New York, 1936.
20. WARNER, William Lloyd, and James C. ABEGGLEN. *Occupational Mobility in American Business and Industry, 1928–1952.* New York, 1955.
21. WOOD, James Playsted. *The Story of Advertising.* New York, 1958.

E. Mining, Transportation, and Lumbering

22. ATHEARN, Robert G. *Rebel of the Rockies: A History of the Denver and Rio Grande Western Railroad.* New Haven, 1962.
23. AUTOMOBILE MANUFACTURERS ASSOCIATION. *Automobiles of America.* Detroit, 1968.

THE AMERICAN AND HIS WORK

1 CLARK, Ira G. *Then Came the Railroads: The Century from Steam to Diesel in the Southwest.* Norman, Okla., 1958.

2 COCHRAN, Thomas C. *Railroad Leaders, 1845–1890: The Business Mind in Action.* New York, 1953.

3 COOTNER, Paul H. "The Role of the Railroads in United States Economic Growth." *J Econ Hist,* XXIII (1963), 477–521.

4 EDWARDS, Charles E. *Dynamics of the United States Automobile Industry.* Columbia, S.C., 1965.

5 ELLIOTT, Russell R. *Nevada's Twentieth-Century Mining Boom: Tonopath; Goldfield; Ely.* Reno, Nev., 1966.

6 EMME, Eugene M. *A History of Space Flight.* New York, 1965.†

7 ENGBERG, George B. "Lumber and Labor in the Lake States," *Minn Hist,* LXV (March 1959), 228.

8 FRIES, Robert F. *Empire in Pine, the Story of Lumbering in Wisconsin, 1830–1900.* Madison, Wis., 1951.

9 GIBB, George Sweet, and Evelyn H. KNOWLTON. *Resurgent Years 1911–1927:* Vol. II of *History of The Standard Oil Company (New Jersey).* New York, 1956.

10 GLAAB, Charles N. *Kansas City and the Railroads: Community Policy in the Growth of a Regional Metropolis.* Madison, Wisc., 1962.

11 GOODRICH, Carter. *Government Promotion of American Canals and Railroads, 1800–1890.* New York, 1960. See 39.3.

12 GORTER, Wytze, and George Herbert HILDEBRAND, Jr. *The Pacific Maritime Shipping Industry, 1930–1948.* 2 vols. Berkeley, 1952–1954.

13 GREENLEAF, William. *Monopoly on Wheels: Henry Ford and the Selden Automobile Patent.* Detroit, 1961.

14 GREEVER, William S. *Arid Domain: The Sante Fe Railway and Its Western Land Grant.* Stanford, 1954.

15 GREEVER, William S. *The Bonanaza West: The Story of the Western Mining Rushes, 1848–1900.* See 14.6.

16 GRISWOLD, Wesley S. *A Work of Giants: Building the First Transcontinental Railroad.* New York, 1962.

17 GRODINSKY, Julius. *Transcontinental Railway Strategy, 1869–1893: A Study of Businessmen.* Philadelphia, 1963.

18 HARVEY, Katherine A. *The Best-Dressed Miners: Life and Labor in the Maryland Coal Region, 1835–1910.* Ithaca, N.Y., 1969.

19 HICKMAN, Nollie. *Mississippi Harvest: Lumbering in the Longleaf Pine Belt, 1840–1915.* University, Miss., 1962.

20 HIDY, Ralph W. et al. *Timber and Men: The Weyerhaeuser Story.* New York, 1964.

21 HIDY, Ralph W. and Muriel E. *Pioneering in Big Business, 1882–1911: Vol I of History of The Standard Oil Company (New Jersey).* New York, 1955.

22 HILTON, George W., and John F. DUE. *The Electric Interurban Railways in America.* Stanford, 1960.

23 HURST, James Willard. *Law and Economic Growth: The Legal History of the Lumber Industry in Wisconsin, 1836–1915.* Cambridge, Mass., 1964.

1 JACKSON, W. Turrentine. *Treasure Hill: Portrait of a Silver Mining Camp.* Tucson, Ariz., 1963.†

2 JENSEN, Vernon H. *Lumber and Labor.* New York, 1945.

3 JOHNSON, Arthur M. *The Development of American Petroleum Pipelines: A Study in Private Enterprise and Public Policy 1862–1906.* Ithaca, N.Y., 1956.

4 JOHNSON, Arthur M. *Petroleum Pipelines and Public Policy, 1906–1959.* Cambridge, Mass., 1967.

5 KENNEDY, E. D. *The Automobile Industry.* New York, 1941.

6 KERR, K. Austin. *American Railroad Politics, 1914–1920.* Pittsburgh, 1968.

7 LORD, Eliot. *Comstock Mining and Miners.* Berkeley, 1959.

8 NEVINS, Allan, and Frank E. HILL. *Ford: The Times, The Man, The Company.* 3 vols. New York, 1952–1963.

9 OVERTON, Richard C. *Burlington West.* New York, 1941.

10 RAE, John B. *The American Automobile: A Brief History.* Chicago, 1965.†

11 RICKARD, T. A. *The History of American Mining.* New York, 1932.

12 SMITH, Duane A. *Rocky Mountain Mining Camps: The Urban Frontier.* Bloomington, 1967.

13 SMITH, Henry L. *Airways: The History of Commercial Aviation in The United States.* New York, 1942.

14 SPENCE, Clark C. *British Investments and the American Mining Frontier, 1860–1901.* Ithaca, N.Y., 1958

15 SPRAGUE, Marshall. *Money Mountain: the Story of Cripple Creek Gold.* Boston, 1953.

16 STOVER, J. F. *American Railroads.* Chicago, 1961.†

17 TAYLOR, George R., and Irene D. NEU. *The American Railroad Network, 1861–1890.* Cambridge, Mass., 1956.

18 WILLIAMSON, Harold F. et al. *The American Petroleum Industry.* 2 vols, Evanston, Ill., 1959–1963.

19 WINTHER, Oscar O. *The Transportation Frontier: Trans-Mississippi West, 1865–1890.* See 14.18.

20 WINTHER, Oscar O. *Via Western Express and Stagecoach.* Lincoln, Neb., 1945.†

F. *Professions, Clerical, and Service*

21 BURROW, James G. *AMA: Voice of American Medicine.* Baltimore, 1963.

22 CALVERT, Monte A. *The Mechanical Engineer in America, 1830–1910: Professional Cultures in Conflict.* Baltimore, 1967.

23 CARSON, Gerald. *The Old Country Store.* New York, 1965.†

1 CLARK, Thomas D. *Pills, Petticoats, and Plows: The Southern Country Store.* See 12.12.

2 EMMET, Boris, and John E. JEUCK. *Catalogues and Counters: A History of Sears, Roebuck and Company.* Chicago, 1950.

3 GILB, Corinne Lathrop. *Hidden Hierarchies: The Professions and Government.* New York, 1966.

4 LEBHAR, Godfrey M. *Chain Stores in America, 1859–1959.* New York, 1959.

5 PACKARD, Vance O. *The Hidden Persuaders.* New York, 1957.†

6 PEASE, Otis. *The Responsibilities of American Advertising: Private Control and Public Influence, 1920–1940.* New Haven, 1958.

7 PERRUCCI, Robert, and Joel E. GERSTL. *Profession Without Community: Engineers in American Society.* New York, 1969.

8 SCHWARTZ, Mildred A. *The United States College-Educated Population, 1960.* Chicago, 1965.

9 Sears, Roebuck and Co. *1897 Sears Roebuck Catalogue.* Chicago, 1968.

10 STIGLER, George J. *Domestic Servants in the United States, 1900–1940.* New York, 1946.

11 TWYMAN, Robert W. *History of Marshall Field and Co., 1852–1906.* Philadelphia, Pa., 1954.

12 U.S. Department of Labor. *How American Buying Habits Change.* Washington, D.C., 1959.

G. Military

13 AMBROSE, Stephen E. *Duty, Honor, Country: A History of West Point.* Baltimore, Md., 1966.

14 BLUM, Albert A. "Soldiers at Work on Farm and in Factory." *SW Soc Sc Q*, XL (1959), 238–244.

15 CARPENTER, John A. *Sword and Olive Branch: Oliver Otis Howard.* See 32.18.

16 COFFMAN, Edward M. "Army Life on the Frontier, 1865–1898." *Mil Affairs*, XX (1956), 193–201.

17 DAVIES, Wallace Evan. *Patriotism on Parade: The Story of Veteran's and Hereditary Organizations in America, 1783–1900.* Cambridge, Mass., 1955.

18 DEARING, Mary R. *Veterans in Politics: The Story of the G.A.R.* Baton Rouge, 1952.

19 FORMAN, Sidney. *West Point: A History of the United States Military Academy.* New York, 1950.

20 FRINK, Maurice, and Casey E. BARTHELMESS. *Photographer on an Army Mule.* New York, 1965.

21 JANOWITZ, Morris. *The Professional Soldier: A Social and Political Portrait.* Glencoe, Ill., 1960.†

1 MATTHEWS, William, and Dixon WECTER. *Our Soldiers Speak, 1775–1918.* Boston, 1943.

2 MOLEY, Raymond, Jr. *The American Legion Story.* New York, 1966.

3 RICKEY, Don, Jr. *Forty Miles a Day on Beans and Hay: The Enlisted Soldier Fighting the Indian Wars.* Norman, Okla., 1963.

4 RIKER, William H. *Soldiers of the States: The Role of the National Guard in American Democracy.* Washington D.C. 1957.

5 STOUFFER, Samuel A. et al. *The American Soldier.* 2 vols, Princeton, 1949.

6 WECTER, Dixon. *When Johnny Comes Marching Home.* Boston, 1944.

H. Labor

1. GENERAL

7 ADAMS, Graham. *Age of Industrial Violence, 1910–15: The Activities and Findings of the U.S. Commission on Industrial Relations.* New York, 1966.

8 ADAMS, Leonard P., and Robert L. ARONSON. *Workers and Industrial Change: A Case Study of Labor Mobility.* New York, 1957.

9 AHEARN, Daniel J., Jr. *The Wages of Farm and Factory Laborers, 1914–1924.* New York, 1945.

10 ALINSKY, Saul D. *John L. Lewis: An Unauthorized Biography.* New York, 1949.

11 ALLEN, Ruth A. *East Texas Lumber Workers: An Economic and Racial Picture, 1870–1950.* Austin, Tex., 1961.

12 ALLSOP, Kenneth. *Hard Travellin': The Hobo and His History.* New York, 1967.

13 AUERBACH, Jerold S. *Labor and Liberty: The LaFollette Committee and the New Deal.* Indianapolis, 1966.

14 BANCROFT, Gertrude. *The American Labor Force: Its Growth and Changing Composition.* New York, 1958.

15 BERNSTEIN, Irving. *The Lean Years: A History of the American Worker, 1920–1933.* Boston, 1960.

16 BROPHY, John. *A Miner's Life: An Autobiography.* Madison, Wis. 1964.

17 BRUCE, Robert V. *1877: Year of Violence.* See 4.7.

18 CHING, Cyrus S. *Review and Reflection: A Half-Century of Labor Relations.* New York, 1953.

19 COMMONS, John R. et al., eds. *A Documentary History of American Industrial Society.* New York, 1909–1911; 1958.

20 COMMONS, John R. et al. *History of Labour in the United States.* 4 vols. New York, 1918–1935.

21 DERBER, Milton, and Edwin YOUNG, eds. *Labor and the New Deal.* See 7.20.

1. DOUGLAS, Paul H. *Real Wages in the United States, 1890–1926.* See 38.19.
2. DULLES, Foster Rhea. *Labor in America, A History.* New York, 1966.†
3. EPSTEIN, Melech. *Jewish Labor in U.S.A., 1914–1952.* New York, 1953.
4. "Fifty Years' Progress of American Labor" *Monthly Labor Rev.*, LXXI (1950), 1–103.
5. FINE, Sidney. *The Automobile Under the Blue Eagle: Labor, Management, and the Automobile Manufacturing Code.* Ann Arbor, Mich., 1963.
6. GARRATY, John A., comp. *Labor and Capital in the Gilded Age: Testimony Taken by the Senate Committee upon the Relations between Labor and Capital, 1883.* New York, 1968.†
7. GINZBERG, Eli, and Hyman BERMAN. *The American Worker in the Twentieth Century: A History through Autobiographies.* New York, 1963.
8. GROB, Gerald N. *Workers and Utopia; A Study of Ideological Conflict in the American Labor Movement, 1865–1900.* Evanston, Ill., 1961.†
9. GUTMAN, Herbert G. "The Worker's Search for Power: Labor in the Gilded Age." *The Gilded Age: A Reappraisal.* Ed. by H. Wayne Morgan. Syracuse, 1963.
10. HARVEY, Katherine A. *The Best-Dressed Miners.* See 45.18.
11. HEALEY, James C. *Foc'sle and Glory Hole: A Study of the Merchant Seaman and His Occupation.* New York, 1936.
12. HOHMAN, Elmo Paul. *History of American Merchant Seamen.* Hamden, Conn., 1956.
13. LAHNE, Herbert J. *The Cotton Mill Worker.* New York, 1944.
14. LAIDLER, Harry Wellington. *How America Lives; A Handbook of Industrial Facts.* New York, 1924.
15. LASSLETT, John, comp. *The Workingman in American Life: Selected Readings.* Boston, 1968.
16. LAYER, Robert G. *Earnings of Cotton Mill Operatives, 1825–1914.* Cambridge, Mass., 1955.†
17. LEIBY, James. *Carroll Wright and Labor Reform: The Origin of Labor Statistics.* Cambridge, Mass., 1960.
18. LESCOHIER, Don D. "Working Conditions." *History of Labor in the United States,* by John R. Commons et al. Vol. III. New York, 1935. pp. 3–396.
19. LEVASSEUR, Emile. *The American Workman.* Trans. by Thomas S. Adams; ed. by Theodore Marburg. Baltimore, 1900.
20. LONG, Clarence D. *The Labor Force in War and Transition.* New York, 1952.
21. LONG, Clarence D. *Wages and Earnings in the United States, 1860–1890.* Princeton, 1960.
22. Mc ENTIRE, Davis. *The Labor Force in California: A Study of Characteristics and Trends in Labor Force, Employment and Occupations in California, 1900–1950.* Berkeley, 1952.†

1. MAN, Albon P., Jr. "Labor Competition and the New York Draft Riots of 1863," *J Neg Hist.* VII (April 1952), 767.
2. MARSHALL, F. Ray. *Labor in the South.* See 13.10.
3. METZ, Harold. *Labor Policy of the Federal Government.* Washington, D.C., 1945.
4. MILLIS, Harry A., and E. C. BROWN. *From the Wagner Act to Taft-Hartley.* Chicago, 1950.
5. MOORE, Wilbert E. *Industrialization and Labor: Social Aspects of Economic Development.* New York, 1965.
6. POTWIN, Marjorie A. *Cotton Mill People of the Piedmont.* See 13.11.
7. REES, Albert. *Real Wages in Manufacturing, 1890–1914.* Princeton, 1961.
8. RISCHIN, Moses. "The Jewish Labor Movement in America: A Social Interpretation." *Lab Hist,* IV (1963), 227–247.
9. SPAHR, Charles B. *America's Working People.* New York, 1900.
10. SWADOS, Harvey. *On the Line.* Boston, 1957.
11. TCHERIKOWER, E., ed. *History of the Jewish Labor Movement in the United States.* New York, 1945.
12. U.S. Bureau of Labor. *Report on Condition of Woman and Child Wage Earners in The United States.* 19 vols. Washington, D.C., 1910–1913.
13. YEARLEY, C. K. *Britons in American Labor, 1820–1914.* Baltimore, 1957.
14. YELLOWITZ, Irwin. *Labor and the Progressive Movement in New York State, 1897–1916.* Ithaca, N.Y., 1965.
15. ZIEGER, Robert H. *Republicans and Labor, 1919–1929.* Lexington, Ky., 1969.

2. LABOR UNIONS

16. BAKER, Elizabeth. *Printers and Technology. A History of the International Printing Pressmen and Assistants Union.* New York, 1957.
17. BERNSTEIN, Irving. "The Growth of American Unions, 1945–60." *Lab Hist,* II (1961), 131–157.
18. BRISSENDEN, Paul F. *The IWW: A Study of American Syndicalism.* New York, 1919; 1957.
19. BRODY, David. *The Butcher Workmen: A Study of Unionization.* Cambridge, Mass., 1964.
20. BRODY, David. *Steelworkers in America: The Nonunion Era.* Cambridge, Mass., 1960.
21. BROEHL, Wayne G. *The Molly Maguires.* Cambridge, Mass., 1964.
22. CHRISTIE, Robert A. *Empire in Wood: A History of the Carpenters' Union.* Ithaca, N.Y., 1956.
23. CONLIN, Joseph R. *Big Bill Haywood and The Radical Union Movement.* Syracuse, 1969.

THE AMERICAN AND HIS WORK

1. DAVIS, Allen F. "The Women's Trade Union League." See 34.21.
2. DUBOFSKY, Melvyn. *We Shall be All: A History of the Industrial Workers of the World.* Chicago, 1969.
3. FONER, Philip S. *History of the Labor Movement in The United States.* 4 vols, New York, 1947–1965.
4. GALENSON, Walter. *The CIO Challenge to the AFL: A History of the American Labor Movement, 1935–1941.* Cambridge, Mass., 1960.
5. GOLDBERG, Arthur J. *AFL-CIO: Labor United.* New York, 1956.
6. GOMPERS, Samuel. *Seventy Years of Life and Labor.* 2 vols. New York, 1925.
7. GREEN, Marguerite. *The National Civic Federation and the American Labor Movement, 1900–1925.* Washington, D.C., 1956.
8. GROB, Gerald N. *Workers and Utopia: A Study of Ideological Conflict in the American Labor Movement, 1865–1900.* See 49.8.
9. GROSSMAN, Jonathan. *William Sylvis, Pioneer of American Labor: A Study of the Labor Movement During the Era of the Civil War.* New York, 1945.
10. HOWE, Irving, and B. J. WIDICK. *The U.A.W. and Walter Reuther.* New York, 1949.
11. JACOBS, Paul. *The State of the Unions.* New York, 1963.
12. JAMES, Ralph and Estelle. *Hoffa and the Teamsters: A Study of Union Power.* New York, 1965.
13. LEITER, Robert D. *The Musicians and Petrillo.* New York, 1953.
14. LEITER, Robert D. *The Teamsters Union: A Study of Its Economic Impact.* New York, 1957.
15. LESTER, Richard A. *As Unions Mature. An Analysis of the Evolution of American Unionism.* Princeton, 1958.†
16. LITWACK, Leon. *The American Labor Movement.* Englewood Cliffs, N.J., 1962.†
17. LORWIN, Lewis L. *The American Federation of Labor; History, Policies, and Prospects.* Washington, D.C., 1933.
18. MADISON, Charles Allan. *American Labor Leaders; Personalities and Forces in the Labor Movement.* New York, 1962.
19. MITCHELL, George S. *Textile Unionism and the South.* Chapel Hill, N.C.. 1931.
20. MORRIS, James O. *Conflict within the AFL: A Study of Craft versus Industrial Unionism, 1901–1938.* Ithaca, N.Y., 1958.
21. NELSON, James. *The Mine Workers' District 50: The Story of the Gas, Coke and Chemical Unions of Massachusetts and Their Growth into a National Union.* New York, 1955.
22. NEUFELD, Maurice F. *A Bibliography of American Labor Union History.* See 2.18.
23. NEWELL, Barbara Warne. *Chicago and the Labor Movement: Metropolitan Unionism in the 1930's.* Urbana, Ill., 1961.
24. PELLING, Henry. *American Labor.* Chicago, 1960.†

1. PERLMAN, Mark. *Labor Union Theories in America: Background and Development.* Evanston, Ill., 1958.
2. PERLMAN, Mark. *The Machinists: A New Study in American Trade Unionism.* Cambridge, Mass., 1961.
3. PERLMAN, Selig. *A History of Trade Unionism in the United States.* New York, 1923.
4. PERLMAN, Selig. *A Theory of The Labor Movement.* New York, 1928.
5. PERRY, Richard S. and Louis B. *A History of the Los Angeles Labor Movement, 1911–1941.* Berkeley. 1963.
6. POWDERLY, Terence V. *The Path I Trod.* New York, 1940.
7. RAYBACK, Joseph G. *A History of American Labor.* New York, 1966.†
8. RENSHAW, Patrick. *The Wobblies: The Story of Syndicalism in the United States.* Garden City, N.Y., 1967.†
9. RICHARDSON, Reed C. *The Locomotive Engineer, 1863–1963: A Century of Railway Labor Relations and Work Rules.* Ann Arbor, Mich., 1963.
10. SAPOSS, David Joseph. *Communism in American Unions.* New York, 1959.
11. SAPOSS, David Joseph. *Left Wing Unionism: A Study of Radical Policies and Tactics.* New York, 1926; 1927.
12. SCHWEPPE, Emma. *The Firemen's and Patrolmen's Unions in the City of New York: A Case Study in Public Employee Unions.* New York, 1948.
13. SEIDMAN, Joel. *American Labor from Defense to Reconversion.* Chicago, 1953.
14. STROUD, Gene S., and Gilbert E. DONAHUE, comps. *Labor History in the United States: A General Bibliography.* See 3.2.
15. TAFT, Philip. *The A. F. of L. in the Time of Gompers.* New York, 1957.
16. TAFT, Philip. *The A. F. of L. from the Death of Gompers to the Merger.* New York, 1959.
17. TAFT, Philip. *Organized Labor in American History.* New York, 1964.
18. TAFT, Philip. *The Structure and Government of Labor Unions.* Cambridge, Mass., 1954.
19. TYLER, Robert L. *Rebels in the Woods: The I.W.W. in the Pacific Northwest.* Eugene, Ore., 1968.
20. WARE, Norman J. *The Labor Movement in the United States, 1860–1895.* New York, 1929.
21. WARNE, Colston E. *Labor in Postwar America.* Brooklyn, 1949.
22. WEINTRAUB Hyman. *Andrew Furuseth: Emancipator of the Seamen.* Berkeley, 1959.
23. WIDICK, B. J. *Labor Today: The Triumphs and Failures of Unionism in the United States.* Boston, 1964.

1 WOLMAN, Leo. *The Clothing Workers of Chicago, 1910–1922.* Chicago, 1922.
2 WOLMAN, Leo. *The Growth of American Trade Unions, 1880–1923.* New York, 1924.

3. STRIKES

3 ANGLE, Paul M. *Bloody Williamson: A Chapter in American Lawlessness.* New York, 1952.
4 BEALS, Carleton. *The Great Revolt and Its Leaders: The History of Popular American Uprisings in the 1890's.* New York, 1968.
5 BRODY, David. *Labor in Crisis: The Steel Strike of 1919.* Philadelphia, 1965.†
6 BRUCE, Robert V. *1877: Year of Violence.* See 4.7.
7 COLEMAN, James Walter. *The Molly Maguire Riots.* Richmond, Ind., 1936.
8 CORNELL, Robert J. *The Anthracite Coal Strike of 1902.* Washington, D.C., 1957.
9 DAVID, Henry. *The History of the Haymarket Affair.* New York, 1936; 1958.†
10 FRIEDHEIM, Robert L. *The Seattle General Strike.* Seattle, 1964.
11 GOULDNER, Alvin W. *Wildcat Strike: A Study in Worker-Management Relationships.* Yellow Springs, Ohio, 1965.†
12 LINDSEY, Almont. *The Pullman Strike.* Chicago, 1942.†
13 Mc MURRY, Donald L. *The Great Burlington Strike of 1888: A Case History in Labor Relations.* Cambridge, Mass., 1956.
14 SMITH, Robert W. *The Coeur d'Alene Mining War of 1892: A Case Study of an Industrial Dispute.* Corvallis, Ore., 1961.
15 WARNER, William Lloyd. *Social System of a Modern Factory. The Strike: A Social Analysis.* New Haven, 1947.
16 WOLFF, Leon. *Lockout: The Story of the Homestead Strike of 1892.* New York, 1965.
17 YELLEN, Samuel. *American Labor Struggles.* New York, 1936.

VII. The American and His Attitude Toward Other Americans

A. *American Character*

18 BELL, Daniel. "Crime as an American Way of Life." *Antioch Rev,* XIII (1953), 131–154.
19 BENSON, Leonard G. *National Purpose: Ideology and Ambivalence in America.* Washington, D.C., 1963.

AMERICAN CHARACTER AND ATTITUDES

1. BROGAN, D. W. *The American Character*. New York, 1956.†
2. BURLINGAME, Roger. *The American Conscience*. New York, 1957.
3. CARSON, Gerald. *The Polite Americans: A Wide-Angle View of Our More or Less Good Manners Over 300 years*. New York, 1966.
4. CHESTER, Edward W. *Europe Views America: A Critical Evaluation*. Washington, D.C., 1962.
5. CURTI, Merle. "American Philanthropy and the National Character." *Am Q*, X (1958), 420–437.
6. DAVIES, Wallace Evan. *Patriotism on Parade*. See 47.17.
7. GORER, Geoffrey. *The American People. A Study in National Character*. New York, 1964.†
8. HOWE, Helen Huntington. *The Gentle Americans, 1864–1960; Biography of a Breed*. See 10.6.
9. LERNER, Max. *America as a Civilization*. See 3.15.
10. LYND, Robert S. and Helen M. *Middletown in Transition*. New York, 1937.†
11. LYND, Robert S. and Helen M. *Middletown*. See 20.17.
12. LYNN, Kenneth S. *The Dream of Success: A Study of the Modern American Imagination*. Boston, 1955.
13. Mc GIFFERT, Michael. "Selected Writings on American National Character and Related Subjects 1969," *Am Q* XXI (Summer 1969), 330–349.
14. MEAD, Margaret. *And Keep Your Powder Dry*. New York, 1942.†
15. MORISON, Elting E., ed. *The American Style: Essays in Value and Performance, A Report on the Dedham Conference of May 23–27, 1957*. See 3.17.
16. NASH, Roderick. *Wilderness and the American Mind*. New Haven, 1967.
17. PETERSEN, William, ed. *American Social Patterns: Studies of Race Relations, Popular Heroes, Voting, Union Democracy, and Government Bureaucracy*. Garden City, N.Y., 1956.
18. POTTER, David M. *People of Plenty: Economic Abundance and the American Character*. Chicago, 1954.†
19. RIESMAN, David. *The Lonely Crowd*. New Haven, 1950.†
20. RISCHIN, Moses, ed. *The American Gospel of Success: Individualism and Beyond*. Chicago, 1965.†
21. SANTAYANA, George. *Character and Opinion in the United States*. New York, 1967.†
22. SCHLESINGER, Arthur M. *Biography of a Nation of Joiners*. New York, 1939.
23. WARD, John William. "The Meaning of Lindbergh's Flight." *Am Q* X (1958), 3–16.
24. WOOLFOLK, George R. *Prairie View: A Study in Public Conscience 1878–1946*. New York, 1962.

B. Public Opinion

1 CORNWELL, Elmer E., Jr. *Presidential Leadership of Public Opinion.* Bloomington, 1965.
2 KLEPPNER, Paul J. *The Cross of Culture.* New York, 1969.
3 LANE, Robert E. *Political Ideology: Why the American Common Man Believes What He Does.* New York, 1962.†
4 ROPER, Elmo B. *You and Your Leaders: Their Actions and Your Reactions, 1936–1956.* New York, 1958.

C. Law and Justice

5 CARTER, Dan T. *Scottsboro: A Tragedy of the American South.* Baton Rouge, 1969.
6 CICOUREL, Aaron V. *The Social Organization of Juvenile Justice.* See 37.16.
7 FOSDICK, Raymond B. *American Police Systems.* New York, 1920.
8 FROST, Richard H. *The Mooney Case.* Stanford, 1968.
9 GARD, Wayne. *Frontier Justice.* Norman, Okla., 1949.
10 GLUECK, Sheldon. *Ten Years of Unraveling Juvenile Delinquency.* New York, 1950.
11 GRISWOLD, Erwin N. *Law and Lawyers in the United States: The Common Law Under Stress.* Cambridge, Mass., 1964.
12 HOWE, Mark Anthony DeWolfe. *Justice Oliver Wendell Holmes.* 2 vols. Cambridge, Mass., 1957–1963.
13 HURST, James Willard. *The Growth of American Law: The Law Makers.* Boston, 1950.
14 HURST, James Willard. *Law and the Conditions of Freedom in the Nineteenth-Century United States.* Madison, Wis., 1956.†
15 LANE, Roger. *Policing the City: Boston 1822–1885.* See 18.18.
16 LERNER, Max, ed. *The Mind and Faith of Justice Holmes.* New York, 1954.
17 MARSHALL, Louis. *Louis Marshall, Champion of Liberty: Selected Papers and Addresses.* Ed. by Charles Reznikoff. Philadelphia, 1957.
18 MASON, Alpheus T. *Brandeis: a Free Man's Life.* New York, 1946.
19 MASON, Alpheus T. *Harlan Fiske Stone: Pillar of the Law.* New York, 1956.
20 MORRIS, Richard B. *Fair Trial: Fourteen Who Stood Accused, From Anne Hutchinson to Alger Hiss.* New York, 1952.†
21 PAUL, Arnold M. *Conservative Crisis and the Rule of Law; Attitudes of Bar and Bench, 1887–1895.* Ithaca, N.Y., 1960.

1. RADANO, Gene. *Walking the Beat: A New York Policeman Tells What It's Like on His Side of the Law.* Cleveland, Ohio, 1968.
2. RUMBLE, Wilfred E., Jr. *American Legal Realism: Skepticism, Reform, and the Judicial Process.* Ithaca, N.Y., 1968.
3. THOMAS, Helen S. *Felix Frankfurter: Scholar on the Bench.* Baltimore, 1960.
4. "U.S. Crime: Its Scope and Causes; A Symposium." *Cur Hist*, LII (June 1967), 321–358.
5. WEBB, Walter P. *The Texas Rangers.* Rev. ed., Austin, Tex., 1965.

D. Civil Liberties

6. BARTH, Alan. *The Loyalty of Free Men; Government by Investigation.* New York, 1951.
7. CARR, R. K. *Federal Protection of Civil Rights, The Quest for a Sword.* Ithaca, N.Y., 1947.
8. CHAFEE, Zechariah, Jr. *Free Speech in the United States.* New York, 1941.
9. COMMAGER, Henry Steele. *Freedom, Loyalty, Dissent.* New York, 1954.
10. DAVIS, Elmer. *But We Were Born Free.* Indianapolis, 1954.
11. HALLGREN, Mauritz Alfred. *Landscape of Freedom; The Story of American Liberty and Bigotry.* New York, 1941.
12. HAND, Learned. *The Bill of Rights.* Cambridge, Mass., 1958.
13. HAND, Learned. *The Spirit of Liberty.* 3d ed. enl. New York, 1960.
14. JOHNSON, Donald. *The Challenge to American Freedoms: World War I and the Rise of the American Civil Liberties Union.* Lexington, Ky., 1963.
15. JOUGHIN, George Louis and Edmund M. MORGAN. *The Legacy of Sacco and Vanzetti.* New York, 1948.
16. KONVITZ, Mitton R. *The Constitution and Civil Rights.* New York, 1947.
17. KONVITZ, Milton R. *Expanding Liberties: Freedom's Gains in Postwar America.* New York, 1966.†
18. Mc MASTER, John B. *The Acquisition of Political, Social, and Industrial Rights of Man in America.* New York, 1903; 1961.
19. PRESTON, William, Jr. *Aliens and Dissenters: Federal Suppression of Radicals, 1903–1933.* New York, 1963.†
20. STOUFFER, Samuel A. *Communism, Conformity and Civil Liberties: A Cross-Section of the Nation Speaks Its Mind.* New York, 1955.†

E. Segregation and Desegregation (See also V E 3)

21. BARRETT, Russell H. *Integration at Ole Miss.* Chicago, 1965.

1 BARTLEY, Numan V. *The Rise of Massive Resistance. Race and Politics in the South During the 1950's.* Baton Rouge, 1969.

2 CORNELY, Paul B. "Segregation and Discrimination in Medical Care in the United States." *Am J Public Health,* XLVI (1956), 1074–1081.

3 FRANKLIN, John Hope. "Jim Crow Goes to School: The Genesis of Legal Segregation in Southern Schools." *S Atl Q,* LVIII (1959), 225–235.

4 GATES, Robbins L. *The Making of Massive Resistance: Virginia's Politics of Public School Degregation, 1954–1956.* Chapel Hill, 1964.

5 HARLAN, Louis R. *Separate and Unequal: Public School Campaigns and Racism in the Southern Seaboard States 1901–1915.* Chapel Hill, 1958.†

6 MUSE, Benjamin. *Ten Years of Prelude: The Story of Integration since the Supreme Court's 1954 Decision.* New York, 1964.

7 NEWBY, I. A. *Challenge to the Court: Social Scientists and The Defense of Segregation, 1945–1966.* Baton Rouge, 1969.

8 SARRATT, Reed. *The Ordeal of Desegregation: The First Decade.* New York, 1966.

9 SMITH, Bob. *They Closed Their Schools: Prince Edward County, Virginia 1951–1964.* Chapel Hill, 1965.†

10 TAEUBER, Karl E. and Alma F. *Negroes in Cities: Residential Segregation and Neighborhood Change.* See 28.12.

11 WIGGINS, Sam P. *The Desegregation Era in Higher Education.* Berkeley, 1966.

F. Nativism, Anti-Semitism, and Anti-Intellectualism

12 ALEXANDER, Charles C. *The Ku Klux Klan in the Southwest.* Lexington, Ky., 1965.

13 BERRY, Brewton. *Race and Ethnic Relations.* 3d ed. Boston, 1965.

14 CHALMERS, David Mark. *Hooded Americanism: The First Century of the Ku Klux Klan, 1865–1965.* Garden City, N.Y., 1965.†

15 DANIELS, Roger. *The Politics of Prejudice: The Anti-Japanese Movement in California and the Struggle for Japanese Exclusion.* New York, 1962.†

16 DAVIES, Wallace Evan. *Patriotism on Parade.* See 47.17.

17 DINNERSTEIN, Leonard. *The Leo Frank Case.* New York, 1968.

18 GATEWOOD, William B., Jr. *Preachers, Pedagogues, and Politicians: The Evolution Controversy in North Carolina, 1920–1927.* Chapel Hill, 1966.

19 GINGER, Ray. *Six Days or Forever? Tennessee v. John Thomas Scopes.* Boston, 1958.

1 HIGHAM, John. *Strangers in the Land.* See 23.4.

2 HOBSON, Laura Z. *Gentlemen's Agreement.* New York, 1947.†

3 HOFSTADTER, Richard. *Anti-Intellectualism in American Life.* New York, 1963.†

4 HYMAN, Harold M. *To Try Men's Souls: Loyalty Tests in American History.* Berkeley, 1959.

5 JACKSON, Kenneth T. *The Ku Klux Klan in the City, 1915-1930.* New York, 1967.

6 KINZER, Donald L. *An Episode in Anti-Catholicism: The American Protective Association.* Seattle, Wash., 1964.

7 LENS, Sidney. *The Futile Crusade: Anti-Communism as American Credo.* Chicago, 1964.

8 MECKLIN, John Moffatt. *The Ku Klux Klan; A Study of the American Mind.* New York, 1924.

9 MURPHY, Paul L. "Source and Nature of Intolerance in the 1920's." *Miss Val Hist Rev*, LI (1964), 60-76.

10 MURRAY, Robert K. *Red Scare: A Study in National Hysteria, 1919-1920.* See 7.2.

11 PRESTON, William, Jr. *Aliens and Dissenters: Federal Suppression of Radicals, 1903-1933.* See 56.19.

12 RANDEL, William Pierce. *The Ku Klux Klan: A Century of Infamy.* Philadelphia, 1965.

VIII. The American and His Religious Life

A. General

13 ABRAMS, Ray A., ed. "Organized Religion in the United States." *Ann Am Acad Pol Soc Sci*, CCLVI (March 1948), vii-172.

14 BRADEN, Charles S. *Spirits in Rebellion; The Rise and Development of New Thought.* Dallas, 1963.

15 BRADEN, Charles S. *These Also Believe: A Study of Modern American Cults and Movements.* New York, 1949.

16 BUTTS, Robert Freeman. *The American Tradition in Religion and Education.* Boston, 1950.

17 CLARK, Elmer T. *The Small Sects in America.* New York, 1949.†

18 CLEBSCH, William A. *From Sacred to Profane America: The Role of Religion in American History.* New York, 1968.†

19 COGLEY, John, ed. *Religion in America.* New York, 1958.†

20 CRAMER, Clarence H. *Royal Bob: The Life of Robert G. Ingersoll.* Indianapolis, 1952.

21 CURRAN, Francis X. *The Churches and the Schools: American Protestantism and Popular Elementary Education.* New York, 1954.

THE AMERICAN AND HIS RELIGIOUS LIFE

1 FREDERIC, Harold. *The Damnation of Theron Ware.* Ed. by Everett Carter. Cambridge, Mass., 1896; 1960.
2 GARRISON, Winfred Ernest. *March of Faith.* New York, 1933.
3 GAUSTAD, Edwin Scott. *A Religious History of America.* New York, 1966.
4 HANDY, Robert T. "The American Religious Depression, 1925–1935." *Church Hist,* XXIX (1960), 3–16.
5 HARLAND, Gordon. *The Thought of Reinhold Niebuhr.* New York, 1960.
6 HARRIS, Sara. *Father Divine, Holy Husband.* New York, 1953.
7 HERBERG, Will. *Protestant, Catholic, Jew: An Essay in American Religious Sociology.* New York, 1960.†
8 HUDSON, Winthrop S. *Religion in America.* New York, 1965.†
9 KEGLEY, Charles W., and R. W. BRETALL, eds. *Reinhold Niebuhr: His Religious, Social and Political Thought.* New York, 1956.†
10 LAMBERT, Richard D., ed., "Religion in American Society." *Ann Am Acad Pol Soc Sci,* CCCXXXII (Nov., 1960), viii–155.
11 Mc LOUGHLIN, William G., and Robert N. BELLAH, eds., *Religion in America.* Boston, 1968.
12 MAKDISI, Nadim. "The Moslems of America." *Christ Cent,* LXXVI (1956), 969–971.
13 MANWARING, David R. *Render unto Caesar: The Flag-Salute Controversy.* Chicago, 1962.
14 MARTY, Martin E. *The New Shape of American Religion.* New York, 1959.
15 MEAD, Sidney. *The Lively Experiment: The Shaping of Christianity in America.* New York, 1963.
16 MUIR, William K., Jr. *Prayer in the Public Schools: Law and Attitude Change.* Chicago, 1968.
17 NICHOLS, Roy F. *Religion and American Democracy.* Baton Rouge, 1959.
18 NIEBUHR, Richard H. *The Kingdom of God in America.* Chicago, 1937.
19 NIEBUHR, Richard H. *The Social Sources of Denominationalism.* New York, 1929.†
20 OLMSTEAD, Clifton E. *History of Religion in the United States.* New York, 1960.
21 "Religion in America." *Daedalus,* XCVI (1967), 1–266.
22 ROY, Ralph Lord. *Communism and the Churches.* New York, 1960.
23 SCHNEIDER, Herbert Wallace. *Religion in Twentieth Century America.* Cambridge, Mass., 1952.†
24 SCHNEIDER, Louis, ed. *Religion, Culture and Society.* New York, 1964.

1 SMITH, James Ward, and A. Leland JAMISON eds. *Religion in American Life.* 4 vols. Princeton, 1961.
2 SWEET, William Warren. *American Culture and Religion: Six Essays.* Dallas, 1951.
3 WARREN, Sidney. *American Freethought, 1860–1914.* New York, 1943.
4 WEISENBURGER Francis P. *Ordeal of Faith: The Crisis of Church-Going America, 1865–1900.* New York, 1959.
5 WEISENBURGER, Francis P. *Triumph of Faith.* Richmond, Va., 1962.
6 WHITE, Edward A. *Science and Religion in American Thought: The Impact of Naturalism.* New York, 1952.

B. The Social Gospel

7 ABELL, Aaron I. *American Catholicism and Social Action: A Search for Social Justice, 1865–1950.* Garden City, N.Y., 1960.†
8 ABELL, Aaron I., comp. *American Catholic Thought on Social Questions.* Indianapolis, 1968.†
9 BROWN, Ira V. *Lyman Abbott, Christian Evolutionist: A Study in Religious Liberalism.* Cambridge, Mass., 1953.
10 BROWNE, Henry J. *The Catholic Church and the Knights of Labor.* Washington, D.C., 1949.
11 CARTER, Paul A. *The Decline and Revival of the Social Gospel, 1920–1940.* Ithaca, N.Y., 1956.
12 CROSS, Robert D., ed. *The Church and the City, 1865–1910.* See 17.13.
13 DORN, Jacob H. *Washington Gladden: Prophet of the Social Gospel.* Columbus, Ohio, 1967.
14 EDDY, Sherwood. *A Century with Youth: A History of the YMCA from 1844 to 1944.* See 37.20.
15 HANDY, Robert T., ed. *The Social Gospel in America.* New York, 1966.
16 HOPKINS, Charles H. *A History of the YMCA in North America.* See 38.1.
17 HOPKINS, Charles H. *The Rise of the Social Gospel in American Protestantism, 1865–1915.* New Haven, 1940.
18 MAY, Henry F. *Protestant Churches and Industrial America.* New York, 1964.†
19 MILLER, Robert Moats. *American Protestantism and Social Issues, 1919–1939.* Chapel Hill, 1958.
20 O'BRIEN, David J. *American Catholics and Social Reform: The New Deal Years.* New York, 1968.
21 RAUSCHENBUSCH, Walter. *Christianity and the Social Crisis.* New York, 1907; 1967.†
22 RYAN, John A. *Social Doctrine in Action. A Personal History.* New York, 1941.

1 SAPPINGTON, Roger E. *Brethren Social Policy, 1908–1958.* Elgin, Ill., 1961.

2 WADE, Louise C. *Graham Taylor: Pioneer for Social Justice, 1851–1938.* Chicago, 1964.

C. Protestants and Protestantism

3 ABELL, Aaron I. *The Urban Impact on American Protestantism, 1865–1900.* Cambridge, Mass., 1943.

4 AHLSTROM, Sydney E., ed. *Theology in America: The Major Protestant Voices from Puritanism to Neo-Orthodoxy.* Indianapolis, 1967.†

5 ALBRIGHT, Raymond W. *A History of the Protestant Episcopal Church.* New York, 1964.

6 ANDERSEN, Arlow W. *The Salt of the Earth: A History of Norwegian-Danish Methodism in America.* Nashville, 1962.

7 ANDREWS, Edward Deming. *The People Called Shakers: A Search for the Perfect Society.* New York, 1953.†

8 ARDEN, G. Everett. *Augustana Heritage: A History of the Augustana Lutheran Church.* Rock Island, Ill., 1963.

9 ARRINGTON, Leonard J. *Great Basin Kingdom: An Economic History of the Latter-Day Saints, 1830–1900.* Cambridge, Mass., 1958.†

10 BAILEY, Kenneth K. *Southern White Protestantism in the Twentieth Century.* New York, 1964.

11 BALTZELL, E. Digby. *The Protestant Establishment: Aristocracy & Caste in America.* New York, 1964.†

12 BRADFORD, Gamaliel. *D. L. Moody, A Worker in Souls.* New York, 1927.

13 BRAUER, Jerald C. *Protestantism in America: A Narrative History.* Philadelphia, 1965.

14 BUCKE, Emory S. et al. *History of American Methodism.* New York, 1964.

15 CARTER, Paul A. *The Decline and Revival of the Social Gospel, 1920–1940.* See 60.11.

16 CARTER, Paul A. "The Fundamentalist Defense of the Faith." *Change and Continuity in Twentieth Century America: The 1920's.* Ed. by John Braeman et al. Columbus, Ohio, 1968.

17 CLARK, Robert D. *The Life of Matthew Simpson.* New York, 1956.

18 CUNNINGHAM, Raymond J. "The Impact of Christian Science on the American Churches, 1880–1910." *Am Hist Rev*, LXXII (1967), 885–905.

19 DAKIN, Edwin Franden. *Mrs. Eddy; The Biography of a Virginal Mind.* New York, 1929.

20 FOSDICK, Harry E. *The Living of These Days.* New York, 1956.†

21 FURNISS, Norman F. *The Fundamentalist Controversy, 1918–1931.* New Haven, 1954.

1. GARRISON, Winfred Ernest, and Alfred T. DE GROOT. *The Disciples of Christ: A History.* St. Louis, 1948.
2. HOSTETLER, John A. *Amish Society.* Baltimore, 1963.†
3. HUDSON, Winthrop S. *American Protestantism.* Chicago, 1961.†
4. Mc LOUGHLIN, William G., Jr. *Billy Graham: Revivalist in a Secular Age.* New York, 1960.
5. Mc LOUGHLIN, William G., Jr. *Billy Sunday was His Real Name.* Chicago, 1955.
6. Mc LOUGHLIN, William G., Jr. *Revivalism: Charles Grandison Finney to Billy Graham.* New York, 1959.
7. MEYER, Donald B. *The Positive Thinkers: A Study of the American Quest for Health, Wealth and Personal Power from Mary Baker Eddy to Norman Vincent Peale.* New York, 1965.†
8. MEYER, Donald B. *The Protestant Search for Political Realism, 1919–1941.* Berkeley, 1960.
9. MULDER, William, and A. Russell MORTENSEN, eds. *Among the Mormons: Historic Accounts by Contemporary Observers.* New York, 1958.
10. MULDER, William. *Homeward to Zion: The Mormon Migration from Scandinavia.* Minneapolis, 1957.
11. NIEBUHR, Reinhold. *Leaves From the Notebook of a Tamed Cynic.* Chicago, 1929.†
12. O'DEA, Thomas F. *The Mormons.* Chicago, 1957.†
13. PEEL, Robert. *Mary Baker Eddy: The Years of Discovery.* New York, 1966.
14. POWELL, Lyman Pierson. *Mary Baker Eddy, A Life Size Portrait.* Boston, 1950.
15. RICE, Charles Scott, and John B. SHENK. *Meet the Amish.* New Brunswick, N.J., 1947.
16. SCHREIBER, William I. *Our Amish Neighbors.* Chicago, 1962.
17. SHAPLEN, Robert. *Free Love and Heavenly Sinners: The Story of the Great Henry Ward Beecher Scandals.* New York, 1954.
18. SMITH, Timothy Lynn. *Called unto Holiness: The Story of the Nazarenes— The Formative Years.* Kansas City, Mo., 1962.
19. SORENSON, Virginia. *Where Nothing is Long Ago: Memories of a Mormon Childhood.* New York, 1963.
20. SPAIN, Rufus B. *At Ease in Zion: Social History of Southern Baptists, 1865–1900.* Nashville, Tenn., 1967.
21. STARKEY, Marion L. *The Congregational Way. The Role of the Pilgrims and Their Heirs in Shaping America.* Garden City, N.Y., 1966.
22. STROUP, Herbert Hewitt. *The Jehovah's Witnesses.* New York, 1945.
23. SWEET, William Warren. *Revivalism in America.* Nashville, Tenn., 1944.†

1 TORBET, Robert G. *A History of the Baptists*, Valley Forge, Pa., 1950.
2 WEISBERGER, Bernard A. *They Gathered at the River: The Story of The Great Revivalists and Their Impact Upon Religion in America.* Boston, 1958.
3 WENTZ, Adbel Ross. *A Basic History of Lutheranism in America.* Gettysburg, 1955.
4 WEST, Ray B. *Kingdom of the Saints: The Story of Brigham Young and the Mormons.* New York, 1957.
5 WILBUR, Earl Morse. *A History of Unitarianism.* 2 vols. Boston, 1965.
6 WITTKE, Carl. *William Nast: Patriarch of German Methodism.* Detroit, 1959.

D. Catholics and Catholicism

7 BARRY, Colman James. *The Catholic Church and German Americans.* Washington, D.C., 1953.
8 CROSS, Robert D. *The Emergence of Liberal Catholicism in America.* Cambridge, Mass., 1958.†
9 ELLIS, John Tracy. *American Catholicism.* Chicago, 1956.†
10 ELLIS, John Tracy. *A Guide to American Catholic History.* Milwaukee, 1959.
11 GREELEY, Andrew M. *The Catholic Experience: An Interpretation of the History of American Catholicism.* Boston, 1967.†
12 Mc AVOY, Thomas T. *The Great Crisis in American Catholic History, 1895-1900.* Chicago, 1957.
13 Mc AVOY, Thomas T. *A History of the Catholic Church in the United States.* Notre Dame, Ind., 1969.
14 Mc AVOY, Thomas T., ed. *Roman Catholicism and the American Way of Life.* Notre Dame, Ind., 1960.
15 Mc CARTHY, Mary. *Memories of a Catholic Girlhood.* New York, 1957.†
16 MAYNARD, Theodore. *The Story of American Catholicism.* New York, 1941.
17 SHIELDS, Currin V. *Democracy and Catholicism in America.* New York, 1958.
18 SWEENEY, David F. *The Life of John Lancaster Spalding: First Bishop of Peoria, 1840-1916.* New York, 1965.

E. Jews and Judaism

19 BERG, Mrs. Harry, and Jacob R. MARCUS, eds. *Jewish Americana.* Cincinnati, 1954.

1. BLAU, Joseph L., and Salo W. BARON, eds. *The Jews of the United States, 1790–1840: A Documentary History*. 3 vols. New York, 1963.

2. BRECK, Allen DuPont. *The Centennial History of the Jews of Colorado, 1859–1959*. Denver, Col., 1960.

3. CRONBACH, Abraham. "Jewish Pioneering in American Social Welfare." *Am Jew Archiv*, Vol. III (1951), 51–80.

4. DAVIS, Moshe. *The Emergence of Conservative Judaism: The Historical School in 19th Century America*. New York, 1963.

5. DE SOLA, David, and Tamar POOL. *An Old Faith in the New World: Portrait of Shearith Israel, 1654–1954*. New York, 1955.

6. GAY, Ruth. *Jews in America: A Short History*. New York, 1965.

7. GLANZ, Rudolf. *The Jews of California from the Discovery of Gold until 1880*. New York, 1960.

8. GLAZER, Nathan. *American Judaism*. Chicago, 1957.†

9. HANDLIN, Oscar. *Adventure in Freedom: Three Hundred Years of Jewish Life in America*. New York, 1954.

10. HELLER, James G. *Isaac M. Wise*. New York, 1965.

11. KISCH, Guido. *In Search of Freedom: A History of American Jews from Czechoslovakia*. London, 1949.

12. KNOX, Israel. *Rabbi in America: The Story of Isaac M. Wise*. Boston, 1957.

13. KRAMER, Judith R., and Seymour LEVENTMAN. *Children of the Gilded Ghetto: Conflict Resolutions of Three Generations of American Jews*. New Haven, 1961.

14. LEARSI, Rufus. *The Jews in America: A History*. Cleveland, 1954.

15. PLAUT, W. Gunther. *The Jews in Minnesota: The First Seventy-Five Years*. New York, 1959.

16. PLAUT, W. Gunther. *The Rise of Reform Judaism*. New York, 1969.

17. RISCHIN, Moses. *An Inventory of American Jewish History*. Cambridge, Mass., 1954.†

18. RISCHIN, Moses. *The Promised City; New York's Jews, 1870–1914*. Cambridge, Mass., 1962.†

19. SHERMAN, C. Bezalel. *The Jew Within American Society: A Study in Ethnic Individuality*. Detroit, 1961.†

20. SKLARE, Marshall, ed. *The Jews: Social Patterns of an American Group*. New York, 1958.

21. SOLOMON, Barbara Miller. *Pioneers in Service: The History of the Associated Jewish Philanthropies of Boston*. Boston, 1956.

22. STEMBER, Charles Herbert et al. *Jews in the Mind of America*. New York, 1966.

23. TELLER, Judd L. *Strangers and Natives: The Evolution of the American Jew from 1921 to the Present*. New York, 1968.

IX. Social and Political Thought

A. General

1 ADDAMS, Jane. *Democracy and Social Ethics.* Cambridge, Mass., 1902; 1964.†

2 ALTGELD, John P. *The Mind and Spirit of John Peter Altgeld: Selected Writings and Addresses.* Ed. by Henry M. Christman. Urbana, Ill., 1960.†

3 BELL, Daniel. *The End of Ideology: On the Exhaustion of Political Ideas in the Fifties.* Glencoe, Ill., 1960.†

4 BELLAMY, Edward. *Looking Backward 2000–1887.* Cambridge, Mass., 1888; 1967.†

5 BOORSTIN, Daniel J. *The Image: Or What Happened to the American Dream.* New York, 1962.†

6 BOWMAN, Sylvia E. *The Year 2000: A Critical Biography of Edward Bellamy.* New York, 1958.

7 BREMNER, Robert H. *From the Depths; The Discovery of Poverty in the United States.* New York, 1956.†

8 BUDD, Louis J. *Mark Twain: Social Philosopher.* Bloomington, 1962.

9 CHALMERS, David Mark. *The Social and Political Ideas of the Muckrakers.* New York, 1964.†

10 COMMAGER, Henry Steele, ed. *Lester Ward and the Welfare State.* Indianapolis, 1967.

11 CURTI, Merle E. *The Social Ideas of American Educators.* Totowa, N.J., 1959.†

12 DESTLER, Chester McArthur. *Henry Demarest Lloyd and Empire of Reform.* Philadelphia, 1963.†

13 DOWD, Douglas F., ed. *Thorstein Veblen.* New York, 1966.†

14 FARRELL, John C. *Beloved Lady: A History of Jane Addams' Ideas on Reform and Peace.* Baltimore, 1967.

15 FINE, Sidney. *Laissez Faire and the General-Welfare State, 1865–1901.* See 5.13.

16 FOX, Daniel M. *The Discovery of Abundance: Simon N. Patten and the Transformation of Social Theory.* Ithaca, N.Y., 1967.

17 GEORGE, Henry. *Progress and Poverty.* New York, 1879.

18 GREENBAUM, Fred. *The Social Ideas of Samuel Gompers.* New York, 1930.

19 GREENE, Lee S., ed., "Conservatism, Liberalism, and National Issues." *Ann Am Acad Pol Soc Sci,* CCCXLIV (Nov., 1962), ix–140.

20 GREER, Thomas H. *American Social Reform Movements; Their Pattern since 1865.* New York, 1949.

1 HALLER, Mark H. *Eugenics: Hereditarian Attitudes in American Thought.* New Brunswick, N.J., 1963.
2 HALTZMAN, Abraham. *The Townsend Movement: A Political Study.* New York, 1963.
3 HEALD, Morrell. "Business Thought in the Twenties: Social Responsibility." *Am Q*, XIII (1961), 126–139.
4 HOFSTADTER, Richard. *Social Darwinism in American Thought.* Philadelphia, 1944.†
5 HOUGH, Robert L. *The Quiet Rebel: William Dean Howells as Social Commentator.* Lincoln, Neb., 1959.
6 JAHER, Frederic Cople. *Doubters and Dissenters: Cataclysmic Thought in America, 1885–1918.* Glencoe, 1964.
7 JAMES, William. *The Varieties of Religious Experience.* New Hyde Park, N.Y., 1902; 1963.†
8 LASCH, Christopher. *The New Radicalism in America.* New York, 1965.†
9 LASCH, Christopher, ed. *The Social Thought of Jane Addams.* Indianapolis, 1965.†
10 LASKI, Harold J. *The American Democracy: A Commentary and an Interpretation.* New York, 1948.
11 LEVINE, Daniel. *Varieties of Reform Thought.* Madison, Wis., 1964.
12 LLOYD, Caroline Augusta. *Henry Demarest Lloyd.* New York, 1912.
13 LLOYD, Henry Demarest. *Wealth Against Commonwealth.* Englewood Cliffs, N.J., 1894; 1963.†
14 MADISON, Charles Allan. *Critics and Crusaders: A Century of American Protest.* New York, 1947.
15 MADISON, Charles Allan. *Leaders and Liberals in 20th Century America.* New York, 1961.
16 MARX, Leo. *The Machine in the Garden: Technology and the Pastoral Ideal in America.* See 19.2.
17 MEIER, August. *Negro Thought in America, 1880–1915: Racial Ideologies in the Age of Booker T. Washington.* See 31.18.
18 MORGAN, Arthur E. *Philosophy of Edward Bellamy.* New York, 1945.†
19 NEWBY, I. A. *Jim Crow's Defense: Anti-Negro Thought in America, 1900–1930.* See 30.16.
20 NOBLE, David W. *The Paradox of Progressive Thought.* Minneapolis, 1958.
21 PAULSON, Ross E. *Radicalism and Reform: The Vrooman Family and American Social Thought, 1837–1937.* Lexington, Ky., 1968.
22 POLLACK, Norman. *The Populist Response to Industrial America: Midwestern Populist Thought.* Cambridge, Mass., 1962.†
23 PROTHRO, James W. *The Dollar Decade: Business Ideas in the 1920's.* See 44.17.

SOCIAL AND POLITICAL THOUGHT

1 RADER, Benjamin G. *The Academic Mind and Reform. The Influence of Richard T. Ely in American Life.* Lexington, Ky., 1966.
2 SCHLESINGER, Arthur M. *The American as Reformer.* Cambridge, Mass., 1950.†
3 SIMONS, A. M. *Social Forces in American History.* New York, 1912.
4 TIPPLE, John O., comp. *Crisis of the American Dream: A History of American Social Thought, 1920–1940.* New York, 1968.†
5 Twelve Southerners. *I'll Take My Stand: The South and The Agrarian Tradition.* See 12.19.
6 WEAVER, Richard M. *The Southern Tradition at Bay: A History of Postbellum Thought.* Ed. by George Core and M. E. Bradford, New Rochelle, N.Y., 1968.
7 WEYL, Walter. *The New Democracy.* New York, 1912.
8 WHITE, Morton G. *Social Thought in America.* New York, 1957.†
9 WYLLIE, Irvin G. "Social Darwinism and the Businessman." *Proc. Am Philos Soc*, CIII (1959), 629–635.
10 ZINN, Howard, ed. *New Deal Thought.* Indianapolis, 1966.†

B. Radicalism

11 ALINSKY, Saul D. *Reveille for Radicals.* Chicago, 1946.
12 BERNSTEIN, Barton J., ed. *Towards a New Past: Dissenting Essays in American History.* New York, 1968.†
13 BRISSENDEN, Paul F. *The IWW: A Study of American Syndicalism.* See 50.18.
14 CAUGHEY, John W. "Their Majesties The Mob." *Pac Hist Rev*, XXVI (1957), 217–234.
15 CONLIN, Joseph R. *Big Bill Haywood and the Radical Union Movement.* See 50.23.
16 DESTLER, Chester McArthur. *American Radicalism, 1865–1901.* New London, Conn., 1966.†
17 DRINNON, Richard. *Rebel in Paradise; A Biography of Emma Goldman.* Chicago, 1961.
18 FROST, Richard H. *The Mooney Case.* See 55.8.
19 GILBERT, James Burkhart. *Writers and Partisans: A History of Literary Radicalism in America.* New York, 1968.
20 GOLDBERG, Harvey, ed. *American Radicals: Some Problems and Personalities.* New York, 1957.
21 HALLGREN, Mauritz Alfred. *Seeds of Revolt.* New York, 1933.
22 JACOBS, Paul, and Saul LANDAU. *The New Radicals.* New York, 1966.†
23 LASCH, Christopher. *The New Radicalism in America.* See 66.8.
24 LENS, Sydney. *Radicalism in America.* New York, 1966.

SOCIAL AND POLITICAL THOUGHT

1 NEWFIELD, Jack. *A Prophetic Minority.* New York, 1966.†
2 RIDEOUT, Walter B. *The Radical Novel in the United States, 1900-1954.* New York, 1956.†
3 SMITH, Gibbs M. *Joe Hill.* Salt Lake City, Utah, 1969.
4 STEFFENS, Lincoln. *The Autobiography of Lincoln Steffens.* 2 vols. New York, 1931.†
5 SYMES, Lillian and Travers CLEMENT. *Rebel America; The Story of Social Revolt in The United States.* New York, 1934.

C. Socialism

6 BELL, Daniel. "Socialism: The Dream and the Reality." *Antioch Rev,* XII (1952), 3-17.
7 EGBERT, Donald D., and Stow PERSONS, eds. *Socialism and American Life.* 2 vols. Princeton, 1952.
8 GINGER, Ray. *The Bending Cross: A Biography of Eugene Victor Debs.* New Brunswick, N.J., 1949.†
9 KIPNIS, Ira. *The American Socialist Movement, 1897-1912.* New York, 1952.
10 LAIDLER, Harry Wellington. *American Socialism; Its Aims and Practical Program.* New York, 1937.
11 LENS, Sidney. *Radicalism in America:* See 67.24.
12 MORGAN, H. Wayne, ed. *American Socialism Nineteen Hundred to Nineteen Sixty.* New York, 1964.†
13 O'NEILL, William L. ed. *Echoes of Revolt: The Masses, 1911-1917.* Chicago, 1966.
14 PELLING, Henry. *America and the British Left: From Bright to Bevan.* New York, 1957.
15 QUINT, Howard H. *The Forging of American Socialism: Origins of the Modern Movement.* Columbia, S.C., 1953.†
16 SHANNON, David A. *The Socialist Party of America: A History.* Chicago, 1967.†
17 WEINSTEIN, James. *The Decline of Socialism in America, 1912-1925.* New York, 1967.
18 YORBURG, Betty. *Utopia and Reality: A Collective Portrait of American Socialists.* New York, 1969.

D. Communism

19 AARON, Daniel. *Writers on the Left: Episodes in American Literary Communism.* New York, 1961.†
20 BELL, Daniel. *Marxian Socialism in the United States.* Princeton, 1967.†
21 BERNSTEIN, Samuel. *The First International in America.* New York, 1962.

SOCIAL AND POLITICAL THOUGHT

1. BROWDER, Earl. "The American Communist Party in the Thirties." *As We Saw the Thirties.* Ed. by Rita Simon. Urbana, Ill., 1967, pp. 216–253.
2. DRAPER, Theodore. *The Roots of American Communism.* New York, 1957.
3. EASTMAN, Max. *Love and Revolution: My Journey Through An Epoch.* New York, 1964.
4. FILENE, Peter G. *Americans and the Soviet Experiment, 1917–1933.* Cambridge, Mass., 1967.
5. FREEMAN, Joseph. *American Testament; A Narrative of Rebels and Romantics.* New York, 1936.
6. GITLOW, Benjamin. *The Whole of Their Lives.* New York, 1948.
7. GLAZER, Nathan. *The Social Basis of American Communism.* New York, 1961.
8. HERRESHOFF, David. *American Disciples of Marx: From the Age of Jackson to the Progressive Era.* Detroit, 1967.
9. HOWE, Irving; Lewis COSER; and Julius JACOBSON. *The American Communist Party: A Critical History (1919–1957).* Boston, 1957.†
10. INVERSON, Robert W. *The Communists and the Schools.* New York, 1959.
11. KEMPTON, Murray. *Part of Our Times.* New York, 1955.†
12. LATHAM, Earl. *The Communist Controversy in Washington: From the New Deal to McCarthy.* Cambridge, Mass., 1962.
13. LYONS, Eugene. *The Red Decade, The Stalinist Penetration of America.* Indianapolis, 1941.
14. RECORD, Wilson. *The Negro and the Communist Party.* See 28.7.
15. RECORD, Wilson. *Race and Radicalism: The NAACP and the Communist Party in Conflict.* See 28.8.
16. ROSSITER, Clinton L. *Marxism: The View from America.* New York, 1960.
17. ROY, Ralph Lord. *Communism and The Churches.* See 59.22.
18. SAPOSS, D. J. *Communism in American Politics.* Washington, 1960.
19. SAPOSS, D. J. *Communism in American Unions.* See 52.10.
20. SHANNON, David A. *The Decline of American Communism. A History of the Communist Party of the United States since 1945.* New York, 1959.
21. WARREN, Frank A., III. *Liberals and Communism: The "Red Decade" Revisited.* Bloomington, 1966.

E. Liberalism

22. AARON, Daniel. *Men of Good Hope, A Story of American Progressives.* New York, 1951.†

1. BAILEY, Hugh C. *Liberalism in the New South: Southern Social Reformers and the Progressive Movement.* Miami, Fla., 1970.
2. CROLY, Herbert. *The Promise of American Life.* New York, 1909; 1965.†
3. DEWEY, John. *Individualism New and Old.* New York, 1930; 1962.†
4. EKIRCH, Arthur A. Jr. *The Decline of American Liberalism.* New York, 1955.†
5. FILLER, Louis. *Muckrakers: Crusaders for American Liberalism.* See 6.15.
6. FORCEY, Charles. *The Crossroads of Liberalism: Croly, Weyl, Lippmann, and the Progressive Era, 1900–1925.* New York, 1961.†
7. HAREVEN, Tamara K. *Eleanor Roosevelt: An American Conscience.* Chicago, 1968.
8. HARTZ, Louis. *The Liberal Tradition in America.* New York, 1955.
9. HOWE, Frederic C. *The Confessions of a Reformer.* New York, 1925.†
10. HUTHMACHER, J. Joseph. *Senator Robert F. Wagner and the Rise of Urban Liberalism.* New York, 1968.
11. HUTHMACHER, J. Joseph. "Urban Liberalism and the Age of Reform." See 18.12.
12. LILIENTHAL, David. *This I Do Believe.* New York, 1949.
13. MADISON, Charles A. *Leaders and Liberals in 20th Century America.* See 66.15.
14. SCHLESINGER, Arthur M. Jr. *The Vital Center.* Boston, 1949.†
15. TRILLING, Lionel. *The Liberal Imagination.* New York, 1950.†
16. WHITLOCK, Brand. *Forty Years of It.* New York, 1970.

F. Conservatism

17. BELL, Daniel, ed. *The Radical Right. The New American Right Expanded and Updated.* Garden City, N.Y., 1963.†
18. BERTHOFF, Rowland Tappan. "The American Social Order: A Conservative Hypothesis." *Am Hist Rev* LXV (1960), 495–514.
19. GUTTMANN, Allen. *The Conservative Tradition in America.* New York, 1967.
20. HART, Jeffrey. *The American Dissent: A Decade of Modern Conservatism.* New York, 1966.
21. KIRK, Russell. *The Conservative Mind, From Burke to Santayana.* Chicago, 1953.†
22. KIRK, Russell. *A Program for Conservatives.* Chicago, 1954.†
23. ROSSITER, Clinton. *Conservatism in America; The Thankless Persuasion.* Rev. ed. New York, 1962.

G. Utopianism

1   BESTOR, Arthur E. *Backwoods Utopias.* Philadelphia, 1950.
2   CONKIN, Paul K. *Two Paths to Utopia: The Hutterites and the Llano Colony.* Lincoln, Neb., 1964.
3   GREENWALT, Emmett A. *The Point Loma Community in California, 1897–1942: A Theosophical Experiment.* Berkeley, 1955.
4   HINE, Robert V. *California's Utopian Colonies.* San Marino, Calif., 1953.†
5   WILSON, William E. *The Angel and the Serpent: The Story of New Harmony.* Bloomington, Ind., 1964.

X. Social Problems and Reform Movements

A. General

6   BEAN, Walton E. *Boss Ruef's San Francisco: The Story of the Union Labor Party, Big Business, and the Graft Prosecution.* Berkeley, 1952.
7   BLODGETT, Geoffrey. *The Gentle Reformers: Massachusetts Democrats in the Cleveland Era.* Cambridge, Mass., 1966.
8   BRANDEIS, Elizabeth. "Labor Legislation." Vol II of *History of Labor in the United States*, by John R. Commons et al. New York, 1935.
9   CHAMBERS, Clarke A. *Seedtime of Reform.* See 7.18.
10 DOAN, Edward. *The La Follettes and the Wisconsin Idea.* New York, 1947.
11 FAULKNER, Harold U. *The Quest for Social Justice, 1898–1914.* See 6.14.
12 FILLER, Louis. *A Dictionary of American Social Reform.* See 1.17.
13 GREER, Thomas H. *American Social Reform Movements: Their Pattern since 1865.* See 65.20.
14 HABER, Samuel. *Efficiency and Uplift: Scientific Management in the Progressive Era, 1890–1920.* See 43.19.
15 Mc FARLAND, Gerald W. "The New York Mugwamps of 1884: A Profile." *Pol Sci Q*, LXXVIII (1963), 40–58.
16 MOWRY, George E. *The California Progressives.* Berkeley, 1951.
17 SCHWARTZ, Harold. *Samuel Gridley Howe, Social Reformer, 1801–1876.* Cambridge, Mass., 1956.
18 SHERMAN, Richard B. "The Status Revolution and Massachusetts Progressive Leadership." *Pol Sci Q*, LXXVIII (1963), 59–65.

SOCIAL PROBLEMS AND REFORM MOVEMENTS

1. TAGER, Jack. "Progressives, Conservatives and the Theory of the Status Revolution." *Mid-Am*, XLVIII (1966), 162–175.
2. WARNER, Hoyt Landon. *Progressivism in Ohio, 1897–1917.* Columbus, Ohio, 1964.

B. Poverty

3. BAGDIKIAN, Ben H. *In the Midst of Plenty: The Poor in America.* Boston, 1964.†
4. BECKER, Dorothy G. "The Visitor to the New York City Poor, 1843–1920." *Soc Svc Rev*, XXXV (1961), 382–396.
5. BOND, Floyd A. et al. *Our Needy Aged.* New York, 1954.
6. BREMNER, Robert H. *From the Depths: The Discovery of Poverty in the United States.* See 65.7.
7. FISHMAN, Leo. *Poverty Amid Affluence.* New Haven, 1966.†
8. HAPGOOD, Hutchins. *The Spirit of the Ghetto.* Cambridge, Mass., 1907; 1967.†
9. HARRINGTON, Michael. *The Other America: Poverty in the United States.* New York, 1962.†
10. Hull-House, Residents of. *Hull-House Maps and Papers.* New York, 1895.
11. HUNTER, Robert. *Poverty.* New York, 1904; 1965.†
12. LARNER, Jeremy and Irving HOWE. *Poverty: Views from the Left.* New York, 1968.†
13. LENS, Sidney. *Poverty, America's Enduring Paradox.* New York, 1969.
14. MILLER, Herman P. *Rich Man, Poor Man.* New York, 1964.†
15. NEUBERGER, Richard L., and Kelly LOE. *An Army of the Aged.* Caldwell, Idaho, 1936.
16. RIIS, Jacob A. *The Battle with the Slums.* New York, 1902.
17. RIIS, Jacob A. *The Children of the Poor.* New York, 1892.
18. RIIS, Jacob A. *How the Other Half Lives.* See 19.14.
19. SELIGMAN, Ben B. *Permanent Poverty: An American Syndrome.* Chicago, 1968.
20. SINCLAIR, Upton Beall. *The Cry for Justice: An Anthology of the Literature of Social Protest.* New York, 1915.
21. "Who Spoke For The Poor? 1880–1914," *Soc Casework*, XLIX (1968), 77–112.
22. U.S. President's National Advisory Commission on Rural Poverty. *Rural Poverty in the United States.* Washington, D.C., 1968.
23. WHITE, C. C., and Ada Morehead HOLLAND. *No Quittin' Sense.* Austin, Texas, 1970.
24. WOODS, Robert Archey. *Americans in Process.* Boston, 1903.
25. WOODS, Robert Archey. *The City Wilderness.* Boston, 1899.

C. Public Welfare and Social Security

1. ABBOTT, Grace. *From Relief to Social Security.* New York, 1942.
2. ALTMEYER, Arthur J. *The Formative Years of Social Security.* Madison, Wis., 1966.
3. ANDERSON, Odin W. *The Uneasy Equilibrium: Private and Public Financing of Health Services in the United States, 1875–1965.* Cambridge, Mass., 1968.
4. BECKER, Joseph M. "Twenty-five Years of Unemployment Insurance: An Experiment in Competitive Collectivism." *Pol Sci Q*, LXXV (1960), 481–499.
5. BORNET, Vaughn Davis. *Welfare in America.* Norman, Okla., 1960.
6. CHARLES, Searle F. *Minister of Relief: Harry Hopkins and the Depression.* Syracuse, 1963.
7. DAVIS, Allen F. "Welfare, Reform and World War I." *Am Q*, XIX (1967), 516–533.
8. DE GRAZIA, Alfred, and Ted GURR. *American Welfare.* New York, 1961.
9. ELIOT, Thomas H. "The Social Security Bill 25 Years After." *Atl Monthly*, CCVI (1960), 72–75.
10. EPSTEIN, Abraham. *Insecurity, A Challenge to America.* New York, 1933.
11. FINE, Sidney. *Laissez Faire and the General-Welfare State: A Study of Conflict in American Thought, 1865–1901.* See 5.13.
12. GILBERT, Charles E. "Policy-Making in Public Welfare: The 1962 Amendments." *Pol Sci Q*, LXXXI (1966), 196–224.
13. LEIBY, James. *Charity and Correction in New Jersey: A History of State Welfare Institutions.* New Brunswick, N.J., 1967.
14. LUBOVE, Roy. *The Struggle for Social Security, 1900–1935.* See 6.20.
15. MENCHER, Samuel. *Poor Law to Poverty Program: Economic Security Policy in Britain and the United States.* Pittsburgh, 1967.
16. SCHLABACH, Theron F. *Edwin E. Witte: Cautious Reformer.* Madison, Wis., 1969.
17. U.S. National Resources Planning Board. Committee on Long-Range Work and Relief Policies. *Security, Work, and Relief Policies.* Washington, 1942.
18. WALLS, Otto F. "A History of Social Welfare in Indiana." *Ind. Mag Hist*, XLV (1940), 383–400.
19. WEINSTEIN, James. "Big Business and the Origins of Workman's Compensation." *Lab Hist*, VIII (1967), 156–174.
20. WITTE, Edwin E. *Development of the Social Security Act.* Madison, Wis. 1963.

74 SOCIAL PROBLEMS AND REFORM MOVEMENTS

1 ZORNOW, William Frank. "State Aid for Indigent Soldiers and Their Families in Florida, 1861-1865." *Fla Hist Q*, XXXIV (1956) 259-265.

2 ZORNOW, William Frank. "Texas State Aid for Indigent Soldiers, 1861-1865." *Mid-Am*, XXXVII (1955), 171-175.

D. Housing

3 BREMNER, Robert H. "The Big Flat, History of a New York Tenement House." *Am Hist Rev*, LXIV (1958), 54-62.

4 CONKIN, Paul K. *Tomorrow a New World: The New Deal Community Program.* Ithaca, N.Y., 1959.

5 DAVIES, Richard O. *Housing Reform During the Truman Administration.* Columbia, Mo., 1966.

6 DE FOREST, Robert W. and Lawrence VEILLER. *The Tenement House Problem.* 2 vols. New York, 1903.

7 FORD, James et al. *Slums and Housing with Special Reference to New York City; History, Conditions, and Policy.* Cambridge, Mass., 1936.

8 FRIEDMAN, Lawrence M. *Government and Slum Housing: A Century of Frustration.* Chicago, 1968.

9 LUBOVE, Roy. *Progressives and the Slums: Tenement House Reform in New York City, 1890-1917.* See 6.21.

E. Delinquency and Correction (See also V J)

10 CARLETON, Mark T. "The Politics of Convict Lease System in Louisiana: 1868-1901." *La Hist*, VIII (1967), 5-25.

11 CONRAD, John P., ed. "The Future of Corrections." *Ann Am Acad Pol Soc Sci*, CCCLXXXI (Jan. 1969), xi-158.

12 GREEN, Fletcher M. "Some Aspects of the Convict Lease System in The Southern States." *Essays in Southern History.* . . . Ed. by Fletcher M. Green. Chapel Hill, 1949.

13 HARRIS, Sara. *Hellhole; The Shocking Story of The Inmates and Life in The New York City House of Detention for Women.* New York, 1967.

14 HELFMAN, Harold M. "The Detroit House of Correction, 1861-74." *Mich Hist*, XXXIV, No. 4 (Dec. 1950), 299-308.

15 HOLMES, William F. "James K. Vardaman and Prison Reform in Mississippi." *J Miss Hist*, XXVII (1965) 229-248.

16 LINDNER Robert M. *Rebel Without a Cause.* New York, 1944.†

17 Mc KELVEY, Blake. *American Prisons.* Chicago, 1936.

18 RANDALL, Edwin T. "Imprisonment for Debt in America: Fact and Fiction." *Miss Val Hist Rev*, XXXIX (1952), 89-102.

19 SCHWARTZ, Louis B. ed. "Crime and the American Penal System." *Ann Am Acad Pol Soc Sci*, CCCXXXIX (Jan. 1962), viii-170.

SOCIAL PROBLEMS AND REFORM MOVEMENTS

1 THRASHER, Frederick M. *The Gang.* Chicago, 1927.†
2 TYLER, Gus, ed. "Combating Organized Crime." *Ann Am Acad Pol Soc Sci,* CCCXLVII (May, 1963), viii–112.
3 WILLARD, Josiah Flint (Josiah Flynt). *My Life.* New York, 1908.

F. Philanthropy and Social Work

4 ADDAMS, Jane. *Twenty Years at Hull House.* See 6.10.
5 ANDREWS, Frank Emerson. *Philanthropic Foundations.* New York, 1956.
6 ANDREWS, Frank Emerson. *Attitudes Toward Giving.* New York, 1953.
7 ANDREWS, Frank Emerson. *Corporation Giving.* New York, 1952.
8 BREMNER, Robert H. *American Philanthropy.* Chicago, 1960.†
9 BREMNER, Robert H. *From the Depths.* See 65.7.
10 BREMNER, Robert H. "The Impact of the Civil War on Philanthropy and Social Welfare." *Civil War Hist,* XII (1966), 293–303.
11 BRUNO, Frank J., and Louis TOWLEY. *Trends in Social Work, 1874–1956: A History Based on the Proceedings of the National Conference of Social Work.* New York, 1957.
12 CURTI, Merle. *American Philanthropy Abroad: A History.* New Brunswick, N.J., 1963.
13 CURTI, Merle. "American Philanthropy and the National Character." *Am Q,* X (1958), 420–437.
14 CURTI, Merle et al. "Anatomy of Giving: Millionaires in the Late 19th Century." *Am Q,* XV (1963), 416–435.
15 CURTI, Merle, and Roderick NASH. *Philanthropy in the Shaping of American Higher Education.* New Brunswick, N.J., 1965.
16 CUTLIP, Scott M. *Fund Raising in the United States: Its Role in America's Philanthropy.* New Brunswick, N.J., 1965.
17 DAVIS, Allen F. *Spearheads for Reform: The Social Settlements and the Progressive Movement, 1890–1914.* New York, 1967.
18 DULLES, Foster Rhea. *The American Red Cross: A History.* New York, 1950.
19 FLEXNER, Abraham. *Funds and Foundations: Their Policies Past and Present.* New York, 1952.
20 FOSDICK, Raymond B. *John D. Rockefeller, Jr.: A Portrait.* New York, 1956.
21 FOSDICK, Raymond B. *The Story of the Rockefeller Foundation.* New York, 1952.
22 FOX, Daniel M. *Engines of Culture: Philanthropy and Art Museums.* Madison, Wis., 1963.
23 GREENLEAF, William. *From the Beginnings: The Early Philanthropies of Henry and Edsel Ford, 1911–1936.* Detroit, 1964.

1. KIGER, Joseph Charles. *Operation of Principles of the Larger Foundations.* New York, 1954.

2. LANKFORD, John. *Congress and the Foundations in the Twentieth Century.* River Falls, Wis., 1964.

3. LEE, Joseph. *Constructive and Preventive Philanthropy.* New York, 1906.

4. LUBOVE, Roy. *The Professional Altruist: The Emergence of Social Work as a Career, 1880–1930.* Cambridge, Mass., 1965.†

5. NEVINS, Allan. *Study in Power; John D. Rockefeller, Industrialist and Philanthropist.* See 44.14.

6. PARKER, Franklin. "George Peabody, Founder of Modern Philanthropy." Ph.D. dissertation, Peabody College, 1966.

7. PUMPHREY, Ralph E., and Muriel W., eds. *The Heritage of American Social Work: Readings in its Philosophical and Institutional Development.* New York, 1961.†

8. Russell Sage Foundation. *Report of the Princeton Conference on the History of Philanthropy in the United States.* New York, 1956.

9. SAVAGE, Howard J. *Fruit of an Impulse: Forty-Five Years of the Carnegie Foundation, 1905–1950.* New York, 1953.

10. SHRYOCK, Richard H. *National Tuberculosis Association, 1904–1954: A Study of the Voluntary Health Movement in the United States.* New York, 1957.

11. SILLS, David L. *The Volunteers: Means and Ends in a National Organization.* Glencoe, Ill., 1957.

12. TRATTNER, Walter I. *Homer Folks: Pioneer in Social Welfare.* See 38.15.

13. WADE, Louise C. *Graham Taylor: Pioneer for Social Justice, 1851–1938.* See 61.2.

14. WARE, Louise. *George Foster Peabody: Banker, Philanthropist, Publicist.* Athens, Ga., 1951.

15. WEAVER, Warren et al. *U.S. Philanthropic Foundations. Their History, Structure, Management and Record.* New York, 1967.

16. WISBEY, Herbert A. Jr. *Soldiers Without Swords: A History of the Salvation Army in the United States.* New York, 1955.

17. WOODROOFE, Kathleen. *From Charity to Social Work in England and the United States.* Toronto, 1962.

G. Prohibition

18. BURNHAM, John C. "New Perspectives on The Prohibition 'Experiment' of the 1920's," *J. Soc Hist* II (1968–69), 51–68.

19. BYRNE, Frank L. *Prophet of Prohibition: Neal Dow and His Crusade.* Madison, Wis., 1961.

20. CALKINS, Raymond. *Substitutes for the Saloon.* Boston, 1901.

SOCIAL PROBLEMS AND REFORM MOVEMENTS

1 CHERRINGTON, Ernest Hurst. *The Evolution of Prohibition in the United States of America.* Westerville, Ohio, 1920.
2 DABNEY, Virginius. *Dry Messiah: The Life of Bishop Cannon.* New York, 1949.
3 EUBANKS, John Evans. *Ben Tillman's Baby: The Dispensary System of South Carolina, 1892-1915.* Augusta, Ga., 1950.
4 GUSFIELD, Joseph R. *Symbolic Crusade: Status, Politics and the American Temperance Movement.* Urbana, Ill., 1963.†
5 KOREN, John. *Economic Aspects of the Liquor Problem.* Boston and New York, 1899.
6 MERZ, Charles. *The Dry Decade.* Garden City, N.Y., 1931.
7 OSTRANDER, G. M. *The Prohibition Movement in California, 1848-1933.* Berkeley, 1957.
8 SELLERS, James Benson. *The Prohibition Movement in Alabama, 1702-1943.* Chapel Hill, 1943.
9 SINCLAIR, Andrew. *Prohibition: The Era of Excess.* New York, 1962.†
10 TIMBERLAKE, James H. *Prohibition and the Progressive Movement, 1900-1920.* Cambridge, Mass., 1963.
11 WHITENER, Daniel Jay. *Prohibition in North Carolina, 1715-1945.* Chapel Hill, 1946.

H. Conservation

12 BATES, J. Leonard. "Fulfilling American Democracy: The Conservation Movement, 1907-1921." *Miss Val Hist Rev*, XLIV (1957), 29-57.
13 CHASE, Stuart. *Rich Land, Poor Land.* New York, 1936.
14 CHASE, Stuart. *The Tragedy of Waste.* New York, 1926.
15 COYLE, David C. *Conservation: An American Story of Conflict and Accomplishment.* New Brunswick, N.J., 1957.
16 HAYS, Samuel P. *Conservation and the Gospel of Efficiency; The Progressive Conservation Movement, 1890-1920.* Cambridge, Mass., 1959.†
17 ISE, John. *Our National Park Policy: A Critical History.* Baltimore, 1961.
18 KING, Judson. *The Conservation Fight: From Theodore Roosevelt to the Tennessee Valley Authority.* Washington, D.C., 1959.
19 Mc GEARY, Martin Nelson. *Gifford Pinchot, Forester Politician.* Princeton, 1960.
20 MARSH, George Perkins. *Man and Nature.* Ed. by David Lowenthal. Cambridge, Mass., 1965.
21 PENICK, James L. *Progressive Politics and Conservation; The Ballinger-Pinchot Affair.* Chicago, 1968.
22 PINCHOT, Gifford. *The Fight for Conservation.* Seattle, 1910; 1967.
23 SWAIN, Donald C. *Wilderness Defender: Horace M. Albright and Conservation.* Chicago, 1970.

XI. Cultural Life in America

A. General Cultural Life

1 BOAS, George. "The Rediscovery of America." *Am Q*, VII (1955), 142–52.
2 BROOKS, Van Wyck. *Makers and Finders; A History of the Writers in America, 1800–1915.* 5 vols. New York, 1936–1952.
3 BUTTS, Robert Freeman, and L. A. CREMIN. *A History of Education in American Culture.* New York, 1953.
4 COMMAGER, Henry Steele. *The American Mind: An Interpretation of American Thought and Character Since the 1880's.* New Haven, 1950.†
5 CURTI, Merle. *The Growth of American Thought.* New York, 1943.
6 JAMES, Henry. *The American Essays.* Ed. by Leon Edel. New York, 1956.†
7 KEPPEL, Frederick Paul, and Robert Luther DUFFUS. *The Arts in American Life.* New York, 1933.
8 KOUWENHOVEN, John A. *Made in America: The Arts in Modern Civilization.* Garden City, N.Y., 1948.
9 LERNER, Max. *America as a Civilization: Life and Thought in the United States Today.* See 3.15.
10 LYNES, Russell. *The Tastemakers.* New York, 1954.†
11 Mc DONALD, William F. *Federal Relief Administration and the Arts. The Origins and Administrative History of Arts Projects of the Works Project Administration.* Columbus, Ohio, 1969.
12 MORISON, Elting. *The American Style: Essays in Value and Performance.* See 3.17.
13 NYE, Russel B. *This almost Chosen People: Essays in the History of American Ideas.* East Lansing, Mich., 1966.
14 OVERMYER, Grace. *Government and the Arts.* New York, 1939.
15 PERSONS, Stow. *American Minds: A History of Ideas.* New York, 1958.†
16 POCHMANN, Henry A. et al. *German Culture in America: Philosophical and Literary Influences, 1600–1900.* Madison, Wis., 1957.
17 SIEGFRIED, Andre. *America Comes of Age: A French Analysis.* New York, 1927; 1968.
18 SPILLER, Robert E. et al., eds. *American Perspectives: The National Self-Image in the Twentieth Century.* Cambridge, Mass., 1961.
19 SPILLER, Robert E. et al. *Literary History of the United States.* See 3.1.
20 STEARNS, Harold E., ed. *America Now. An Inquiry into Civilization in the United States by Thirty-Six Americans.* New York, 1938.

1 STEARNS, Harold E., ed. *Civilization in the United States: An Inquiry by Thirty Americans.* See 8.23.
2 VANDERBILT, Kermit. *Charles Eliot Norton: Apostle of Culture in a Democracy.* Cambridge, Mass., 1959.
3 WARNER, William Lloyd. *American Life: Dream and Reality.* Chicago, 1953.†

B. Art, Architecture, and Music

4 ANDREWS, Wayne. *Architecture, Ambition and Americans.* New York, 1955.†
5 BARKER, Virgil. *American Painting, History and Interpretation.* New York, 1950.
6 BAUR, John I. H. *Revolution and Tradition in Modern American Art.* New York, 1965.†
7 BILLINGTON, Ray Allen. "Goverment and the Arts: The W.P.A. Experience." *Am Q*, XIII (1961), 466–479.
8 BLESH, Rudi, and Harriet JANIS. *They All Played Ragtime.* New York, 1950.†
9 BROOKS, Van Wyck. *John Sloan. A Painter's Life.* New York, 1955.
10 BURCHARD, John, and Albert BUSH-BROWN. *The Architecture of America: A Social and Cultural History.* Boston, 1961.†
11 CAHILL, Holger, and A. H. BARR, Jr. *Art in America; A Complete Survey.* New York, 1935.
12 CONDIT, Carl W. *American Building: Materials and Techniques from the First Colonial Settlements to the Present.* Chicago, 1968.
13 CONDIT, Carl W. *The Chicago School of Architecture.* Chicago, 1964.
14 COPLAND, Aaron. *The New Music, 1900–1966.* New York, 1968.
15 Editors of *Art in America*, comps. *The Artist in America.* New York, 1967.
16 ELIOT, Alexander. *Three Hundred Years of American Painting.* New York, 1957.
17 FABOS, Julius G. et al. *Frederick Law Olmsted, Sr.: Founder of Landscape Architecture in America.* Amherst, 1968.
18 FITCH, James M. *American Building.* Boston, 1966.
19 FLEXNER, James T. *That Wilder Image: The Painting of America's Native School from Thomas Cole to Winslow Homer.* Boston, 1962.
20 GOODRICH, Lloyd. *John Sloan.* New York, 1952.
21 GOODRICH, Lloyd. *Thomas Eakins.* New York, 1933.
22 GOODRICH, Lloyd. *Three Centuries of American Art.* New York, 1966.
23 GOODRICH, Lloyd. *Winslow Homer.* New York, 1944.

1 GOODRICH, Lloyd, and John I. H. BAUR. *American Art of Our Century.* New York, 1961.
2 GOWANS, Alan. *Images of American Living: Four Centuries of Architecture and Furniture as Cultural Expression.* Philadelphia, 1964.
3 HITCHCOCK, Henry-Russell. *The Architecture of H. H. Richardson and His Times.* Rev. ed., Cambridge, Mass., 1961.†
4 HITCHCOCK, Henry-Russell. *In the Nature of Materials, 1887–1941; The Buildings of Frank Lloyd Wright.* New York, 1942.
5 HITCHCOCK, H. Wiley. *Music in the United States: A Historical Introduction.* Englewood Cliffs, N.J., 1969.
6 HOWARD, John Tasker. *Modern Music.* New York, 1957.
7 HOWARD, John Tasker. *Our American Music.* 4th ed. New York, 1965.
8 HOWARD, John Tasker. *Our Contemporary Composers; American Music in the Twentieth Century.* New York, 1941.
9 HOWE, Mark Anthony DeWolfe. *Boston Symphony Orchestra.* Boston, 1931.
10 KOLODIN, Irving. *The Metropolitan Opera, 1883–1966; A Candid History.* 4th ed.. New York, 1967.
11 KORNWOLF, James D. *A History of American Dwellings.* Chicago, 1967.†
12 KOUWENHOVEN, John A. *Made in America: The Arts in Modern Civilization.* See 78.8.
13 LARKIN, O. W. *Art and Life in America.* New York, 1949.
14 LEONARD, Neil. *Jazz and the White Americans: The Acceptance of a New Art Form.* Chicago, 1962.
15 LEVY, Lester S. *Grace Notes in American History: Popular Sheet Music from 1820–1900.* Norman, Okla., 1967.
16 LOMAX, John A., ed. *Cowboy Songs and Other Frontier Ballads.* New York, 1910.
17 Mc COUBREY, John W. *American Tradition in Painting.* New York, 1963.
18 MATTFELD, Julius, comp. *Variety Music Cavalcade, 1620–1961.* Englewood Cliffs, N.J., 1962.
19 MEEKS, Carroll L. V. *The Railroad Station: An Architectural History.* New Haven, 1956.
20 MELLQUIST, Jerome. *The Emergence of an American Art.* New York, 1942.
21 MENDELOWITZ, Daniel M. *A History of American Art.* New York, 1960.
22 MOONEY, Hughson F. "Songs, Singers, and Society, 1890–1954." *Am Q,* VI (1954), 221–32.
23 MUELLER, John H. *The American Symphony Orchestra: A Social History of Musical Taste.* New York, 1951.

1. MUMFORD, Lewis. *The Brown Decades: A Study of the Arts in America, 1865–1895.* See 6.2.
2. MUMFORD, Lewis. *Sticks and Stones: A Study of American Architecture and Civilization.* New York, 1955.†
3. OVERMYER, Grace. *Government and Arts.* See 78.14.
4. PICKERING, Ernest. *The Homes of America as They Have Expressed the Lives of Our People for Three Centuries.* New York, 1951.
5. PIERSON, William H. Jr., and Martha DAVIDSON, eds. *Arts of the United States: A Pictorial Survey.* Athens, Ga., 1960.
6. REED, Walt, ed. *The Illustrator in America, 1900–1960's.* New York, 1967.
7. RICHARDSON, Edgar P. *Painting in America: The Story of 450 Years.* New York, 1956.†
8. ROBSJOHN-GIBBINGS, Terence Harold. *Homes of the Brave.* New York, 1954.
9. RODMAN, Selden. *Horace Pippin, A Negro Painter in America.* New York, 1947.
10. RODMAN, Selden. *Portrait of the Artist as an American; Ben Shahn.* New York, 1951.
11. ROSE, Barbara, comp. *Readings in American Art Since 1900; A Documentary Survey.* New York, 1968.†
12. ROSENBERG, Bernard, and Norris E. FLIEGEL. "The Vanguard Artist in New York." *Soc Res,* XXXII (1965), 141–62.
13. SABLOSKY, Irving. *American Music.* Chicago, 1969.†
14. SCHNIER, Jacques. *Sculpture in Modern America.* Berkeley, 1948.
15. SCHULLER, Gunther. *The History of Jazz.* New York, 1968.
16. SCHUYLER, Montgomery. *American Architecture.* New York, 1892; 1965.†
17. SCOTT, John A. *The Ballad of America: The History of the United States in Song and Story.* New York, 1966.
18. SLOAN, John. *John Sloan's New York Scene. From the Diaries, Notes and Correspondence 1906–1913.* New York, 1965.
19. STEARNS, Marshall W. *The Story of Jazz.* New York, 1956.†
20. SULLIVAN, Louis H. *Autobiography of an Idea.* New York, 1924.†
21. TAFT, Robert. *Artists and Illustrators of the Old West, 1850–1900.* See 14.14.
22. THOMSON, Virgil. *Virgil Thomson.* New York, 1966.
23. TRACHTENBERG, Alan. *Brooklyn Bridge: Fact and Symbol.* New York, 1965.
24. ULANOV, Barry. *A History of Jazz in America.* New York, 1952.†
25. WALLACE, David H. *John Rogers: The People's Sculptor.* Middletown, Conn., 1967.

1. WILKINS, Thurman. *Thomas Moran: Artist of the Mountains.* Norman, Okla., 1966.
2. WITTKE, Carl. *The First Fifty Years: The Cleveland Museum of Art, 1916–1966.* Cleveland, 1966.
3. WRIGHT, Frank Lloyd. *An Autobiography.* New York, 1943.
4. WRIGHT, Frank Lloyd. *When Democracy Builds.* New York, 1945.

C. Language, Literature, and Drama

5. AARON, Daniel. *Writers on the Left.* See 68.19
6. BERTHOFF, Warner. *The Ferment of Realism: American Literature, 1884–1919.* New York, 1965.
7. BIER, Jesse. *The Rise and Fall of American Humor.* New York, 1968.
8. BIKLE, Lucy Leffingwell. *George W. Cable: His Life and Letters.* New York, 1928.
9. BLUM, Daniel, ed. *A Pictorial History of The American Theater.* New York, 1951.
10. BUDD, Louis J. *Mark Twain: Social Philosopher.* Bloomington, 1962.
11. CARTER, Everett. *Howells and the Age of Realism.* New York, 1954.
12. CLARK, B. H. *Eugene O'Neill: The Man and His Plays.* New York, 1947.†
13. CROWDER, Richard. *Those Innocent Years: The Legacy and Inheritance of a Hero of the Victorian Era, James Whitcomb Riley.* Indianapolis, 1957.
14. DUNCAN, Hugh D. *The Rise of Chicago as a Literary Center from 1885 to 1920: A Sociological Essay in American Culture.* Tatowa, N.J., 1964.
15. EWEN, David. *The Story of America's Musical Theater.* Philadelphia, 1968.
16. FELHEIM, Marvin. *The Theatre of Augustin Daly: An Account of the Late Nineteenth Century American Stage.* Cambridge, Mass., 1956.
17. FUSSELL, Edwin. *Frontier: American Literature and the American West.* See 14.5.
18. GILBERT, James Burkhart. *Writers and Partisans: A History of Literary Radicalism in America.* See 67.19.
19. HART, James D. *The Oxford Companion to American Literature.* See 2.3.
20. HART, James D. *The Popular Book, A History of America's Literary Taste.* New York, 1950.†
21. HEWITT, Bernard. *Theatre U.S.A., 1668 to 1957.* New York, 1959.

1 HICKS, Granville. *The Great Tradition: An Interpretation of American Literature Since the Civil War.* New York, 1935.†

2 HOFFMAN, Frederick J. *The Twenties: American Writing in the Postwar Decade.* New York, 1955.†

3 HUBBELL, Jay B. *The South in American Literature, 1607–1900.* Durham, N.C., 1954.

4 HUGHES, Glenn. *A History of the American Theatre, 1700–1950.* New York, 1951.

5 JACOBS, Lewis. *The Rise of the American Film.* New York, 1939.

6 JONES, Howard Mumford. *Guide to American Literature and Its Backgrounds Since 1890.* See 2.8.

7 KAPLAN, Justin. *Mr. Clemens and Mark Twain.* New York, 1966.†

8 KAZIN, Alfred. *On Native Grounds.* New York, 1942.†

9 KINNE, Wisner P. *George Pierce Baker and the American Theatre.* Cambridge, Mass., 1954.

10 LAHUE, Kalton C. *World of Laughter: The Motion Picture Comedy Short, 1910–1930.* Norman, Okla., 1966.

11 Mc DONALD, William F. *Federal Relief Adminstration and The Arts. The Origins and Administrative History of Arts Projects of The Works Project Administration.* See 78.11.

12 MATHEWS, Jane De Hart. *The Federal Theatre, 1935–1939: Plays, Relief, and Politics.* Princeton, 1967.

13 MATTHIESSEN, F. O. *Henry James, The Major Phase.* New York, 1944.†

14 MATTHIESSEN, F. O. *Theodore Dreiser.* New York, 1951.

15 MAY, Henry F. *The End of American Innocence: A Study of the First Years of Our Own Time, 1912–1917.* New York, 1959.†

16 MENCKEN, H. L. *The American Language.* Rev. ed. New York, 1936; Supplement I–II, New York, 1945–1948.

17 MEYER, Roy W. *The Middle Western Farm Novel in the Twentieth Century.* Lincoln, Nebr., 1965.

18 MIZENER, Arthur. *The Far Side of Paradise. A Biography of F. Scott Fitzgerald.* Boston, 1965.

19 MORRIS, Lloyd R. *Curtain Time; The Story of The American Theater.* New York, 1953.

20 MOSES, Montrose J., and John M. BROWN, eds. *The American Theatre as Seen by Its Critics, 1752–1934.* New York, 1934.

21 NIETZ, John A. *Old Textbooks: Spelling, Grammar, Reading, Arithmetic, Geography, American History, Civil Government, Physiology, Penmanship, Art, Music—As Taught in the Common Schools from Colonial Days to 1900.* Pittsburgh, 1961.

22 NOWELL, Elizabeth. *Thomas Wolfe.* Garden City, N.Y., 1960.

23 QUINN, Arthur H. *A History of the American Drama.* Rev. ed. New York, 1943.

24 RIDEOUT, Walter B. *The Radical Novel in the United States.* See 68.2.

1 ROURKE, Constance. *American Humor: A Study in the National Character.* New York, 1953.

2 RUBIN, Louis D. Jr., and Robert D. JACOBS, eds. *Southern Renascence: The Literature of the Modern South.* Baltimore, 1953.†

3 SANDBURG, Carl. *Always the Young Strangers.* New York, 1952.

4 SCHICKEL, Richard. *Movies: The History of an Art and an Institution.* New York, 1965.

5 SCHORER, Mark. *Sinclair Lewis: An American Life.* New York, 1961.†

6 TURNBULL, Andrew. *Scott Fitzgerald.* New York, 1962.†

7 VAIL, Henry Hobart. *A History of the McGuffey Readers.* Cleveland, 1910.

8 WECTER, Dixon. *Sam Clemens of Hannibal.* Boston, 1952.†

9 WILSON, Edmund. *The American Earthquake, A Documentary of The Twenties and Thirties.* Garden City, N.Y., 1958.

10 WILSON, Edmund. *The Bit Between My Teeth; A Literary Chronicle of 1950–1965.* New York, 1965.

11 WILSON, Edmund. *Classics and Commercials; A Literary Chronicle of the Forties.* New York, 1950.

12 WILSON, Edmund. *Patriotic Gore; Studies in the Literature of The American Civil War.* New York, 1962.

13 WILSON, Edmund. *The Shores of Light; A Literary Chronicle of the Twenties and Thirties.* New York, 1952.†

14 WRIGHT, Lyle H. *American Fiction, 1851–1875: A Contribution toward a Bibliography.* See 3.6.

D. Popular Culture

15 BARNETT, James H. *The American Christmas: A Study in National Culture.* New York, 1954.

16 CROWTHER, Bosley. *The Great Films: Fifty Golden Years of Motion Pictures.* New York, 1967.

17 DENNEY, Reuel. "The Discovery of Popular Culture." *American Perspectives.* Ed. by Robert E. Spiller and Eric Larrabee. Cambridge, Mass., 1961.

18 GILBERT, Douglas. *American Vaudeville: Its Life and Times.* New York, 1940.†

19 GOULD, Joseph E. *The Chautauqua Movement: An Episode in the Continuing American Revolution.* New York, 1961.†

20 HARRISON, Harry P. *Culture under Canvas: The Story of Tent Chautauqua as Told to Karl Detzer.* New York, 1958.

21 HAUSDORFF, Don. "Magazine Humor and Popular Morality, 1929–34." *Jour Q*, XLI (1964), 509–516.

22 HORNER, Charles F. *Strike the Tents: The Story of the Chautauqua.* Philadelphia, 1954.

1. JACOBS, Lewis. *The Rise of The American Film, A Critical History.* New York, 1939.†
2. JACOBS, Norman et al. "Mass Culture and Mass Media." *Daedalus,* LXXXIX (1960), 271–418.
3. JOHANNSEN, Albert. *House of Beadle and Adams and Its Dime and Nickle Novels.* 3 vols. Norman, Okla., 1962.
4. LYNN, Kenneth S. *The Comic Tradition in America: An Anthology.* New York, 1958.†
5. MAC DONALD, Dwight. *Masscult and Midcult.* New York, 1961.†
6. MURRELL, William. *A History of American Graphic Humor.* 2 vols. New York, 1938.
7. RICHMOND, Rebecca. *Chautauqua, an American Place.* New York, 1943.
8. ROSENBERG, Bernard, and D. M. WHITE, eds. *Mass Culture.* New York, 1957.†
9. SELDES, G. V. *Seven Lively Arts.* New York, 1924; 1962.†
10. SMITH, Henry Nash. *Popular Culture and Industrialism, 1865–1890.* New York, 1967.
11. TAYLOR, Deems et al. *A Pictorial History of The Movies.* New York, 1943.
12. THORP, Margaret F. *American at The Movies.* New Haven, 1939.†

E. Folklore and Folk Culture

13. CAHILL, Holger. *American Folk Art, The Art of The Common Man, 1750–1900.* New York, 1932.
14. COFFIN, Tristam P. "Folklore in the American Twentieth Century." *Am Q,* XIII (1961), 526–533.
15. DORSON, Richard M. *American Folklore.* Chicago, 1959.†
16. DORSON, Richard M. *Buying the Wind: Regional Folklore in the United States.* Chicago, 1964.
17. KNIGHT, Arthur. *The Liveliest Art: A Panoramic History of The Movies.* New York, 1957.†
18. KRAMER, Frank R. *Voices in the Valley: Mythmaking and Folk Belief in the Shaping of the Middle West.* Madison, Wis., 1964.
19. POUND, Louise. *Nebraska Folklore.* Linclon, Neb., 1959.
20. STECKMESSER, Kent Ladd. *The Western Hero in History and Legend.* Norman, Okla., 1965.
21. WOLFE, Tom. *The Kandy-Kolored Tangerine Flake Streamline Baby.* New York, 1963.†

F. Recreation and Sports

22. BETTS, John R. "The Technological Revolution and the Rise of Sport, 1850–1900." *Miss Val Hist Rev,* XL (1953), 231–256.

1 BOATWRIGHT, Mody C. *The American Rodeo.* Lincoln, Nebr., 1959.
2 CARLSON, Reynold E., Theodore R. DEPPE, and Janet R. MacLEAN. *Recreation in American Life.* Belmont, Calif., 1963.
3 COZENS, Frederick W., and Florence Scovil STUMPF. *Sports in American Life.* Chicago, 1953.
4 DULLES, Foster Rhea. *A History of Recreation: America Learns to Play.* Rev. ed. New York, 1965.
5 GALLICO, Paul. *Farewell to Sport.* New York, 1938.
6 HARTT, Rollin Lynde. *The People at Play.* Boston and New York, 1909.
7 JOHNSTON, Alexander. *Ten—and Out! The Complete Story of the Prize Ring in America.* 3d ed. New York, 1947.
8 KROUT, John A. *Annals of American Sport.* New Haven, 1929.
9 Mc CLINTOCK, Inez and Marshall. *Toys in America.* Washington, D.C., 1961.
10 Mc GRAW, J. J. *My Thirty Years in Baseball.* New York, 1923.
11 PLIMPTON, George. *Paper Lion.* New York, 1966.†
12 REDLICH, Fritz. "Leisure-Time Activities: A Historical, Sociological and Economic Analysis." *Explor Entrep Hist,* III (1965), 3–23.
13 RIESMAN, David, and Reuel DENNEY. "Football in America: A Study in Culture Diffusion." *Am Q,* III (1951), 309–325.
14 SEYMOUR, Harold. *Baseball: The Early Years.* New York, 1960.
15 SMITH, Robert. *Baseball. A Historical Narrative of the Game.* New York, 1947.
16 VOIGT, David. *American Baseball: From Gentleman's Sport to the Commissioner System.* Norman, Okla., 1966.
17 WALLACE, Irving. *The Fabulous Showman: The Life and Times of P. T Barnum.* New York, 1959.
18 WIND, Herbert W. *The Story of American Golf.* New York, 1947.

XII. Education and Intellectual Trends

A. General

19 BRICKMAN, William W. *Guide to Research in Educational History.* New York, 1949.
20 CARTWRIGHT, Morse A. "History of Adult Education in the United States." *J Neg Educ,* XIV (1945), 283–292.
21 CURTI, Merle. *The Social Ideas of American Educators, With a New Chapter on the Last Twenty-Five Years.* New York, 1959.
22 DEWEY, John. *Democracy and Education.* New York, 1916.†

EDUCATION AND INTELLECTUAL TRENDS

1 DEWEY, John. *The School and Society.* Chicago, 1899.
2 KANDEL, Isaac L. *American Education in the Twentieth Century.* Cambridge, Mass., 1957.
3 KNIGHT, E. W. *Public Education in the South.* Boston, 1922.
4 Mc CLUSKEY, Neil G., ed. *Catholic Education in America, A Documentary History.* New York, 1964.
5 Mc CLUSKEY, Neil G. *Public Schools and Moral Education: The Influence of Horace Mann, William Torrey Harris and John Dewey.* New York, 1958.
6 MUIR, William K. Jr., *Prayer in the Public Schools: Law and Attitude Change* See 59.16.
7 NOBLE, Stuart G. *History of American Education.* New York, 1954.
8 RICKOVER, Hyman G. *Education and Freedom.* New York, 1959.†
9 WELTER, Rush. *Popular Education and Democratic Thought in America.* New York, 1962.†
10 WESLEY, Edgar B. *NEA: The First Hundred Years—The Building of the Teaching Profession.* New York, 1957.

B. Elementary and Secondary

11 ASHBURN, Frank D. *Peabody of Groton, a Portrait.* New York, 1944.
12 BESTOR, Arthur E. *Educational Wastelands; The Retreat from Learning in our Public Schools.* Urbana, Ill., 1953.
13 BESTOR, Arthur E. *The Restoration of Learning.* New York, 1955.
14 COHEN, Sol. *Progressive Urban School Reform.* New York, 1964.
15 CONANT, James Bryant. *Slums and Suburbs.* New York, 1961.
16 CREMIN, Lawrence A. *The Transformation of the School: Progressivism in American Education, 1876-1957.* New York, 1961.†
17 ELSON, Ruth Miller. *Guardians of Tradition: American Schoolbooks of the Nineteenth Century.* Lincoln, Neb., 1964.
18 GRAHAM, Patricia Albjerg. *Progressive Education: From Arcady to Academe. A History of the Progressive Education Association, 1919-1955.* New York, 1967.
19 HARLAN, Louis R. *Separate But Unequal.* See 31.14.
20 KRUG, Edward Augustus. *The Shaping of the American High School.* New York, 1964.
21 ORR, Oliver H., Jr. *Charles Brantley Aycock.* Chapel Hill, 1961.
22 SIZER, Theodore R. *Secondary Schools at the Turn of the Century.* New Haven, 1964.
23 TYACK, David B. "Bureaucracy and the Common School: The Example of Portland, Oregon, 1851-1913," *Am Q* XIX (Fall 1967), 475-498.

EDUCATION AND INTELLECTUAL TRENDS

1 TYACK, David B. "The Perils of Pluralism: The Backgrounds of the Pierce Case," *Am Hist Rev* LXXIV (Oct. 1968), 74–98.
2 WOODRING, Paul. *A Fourth of a Nation.* New York, 1957.

C. Higher Education

3 ALLEN, Herman R. *Open Door to Learning: The Land-Grant System enters Its Second Century.* Urbana, Ill., 1963.
4 AMBROSE, Stephen E. *Duty, Honor, Country: A History of West Point.* See 47.13.
5 BABBIDGE, Homer D. Jr., and Robert M. ROSEMZWEIG. *The Federal Interest in Higher Education.* New York, 1962.
6 BARNARD, John. *From Evangelicalism to Progressivism at Oberlin College, 1866–1917.* Columbus, Ohio, 1969.
7 BELL, Daniel, and Irving KRISTOL, eds., *Confrontation; The Student Rebellion and The Universities.* New York, 1969.
8 BERELSON, Bernard. *Graduate Education in the United States.* New York, 1960.
9 BISHOP, Morris. *A History of Cornell.* Ithaca, N.Y., 1962.
10 BLEGEN, Theodore C. *Minnesota: A History of the State University o, Minnesota.* Minneapolis, Minn., 1963.
11 BRITTAIN, Marion Luther. *The Story of Georgia Tech.* Chapel Hill, 1948.
12 BROOKS, Robert P. *The University of Georgia under Sixteen Administrations. 1785–1955.* Athens, Ga., 1956.
13 BROWN, Elizabeth G. and William Wirt BLUME. *Legal Education at Michigan, 1859–1959.* Ann Arbor, 1959.
14 CARY, Harold W. *The University of Massachusetts: A History of One Hundred Years.* Amherst, 1962.
15 CHAFFIN, N. C. *Trinity College, 1839–1892: The Beginnings of Duke University.* Durham, N.C., 1950.
16 CHESNEY, Alan M. *The Johns Hopkins Hospital and the Johns Hopkins University School of Medicine: A Chronicle.* 3 vols. Baltimore, 1958.
17 CHESSMAN, G. Wallace. *Denison: The Story of an Ohio College.* Granville, Ohio, 1957.
18 CHEYNEY, E. P. *History of the University of Pennsylvania, 1740–1940.* Philadelphia, 1940.
19 COLE, Arthur Charles. *A Hundred Years of Mount Holyoke College.* New Haven, 1940.
20 COLMAN, Gould P. *Education and Agriculture: A History of the New York State College of Agriculture at Cornell University.* Ithaca, N.Y., 1963.
21 COON, Horace. *Columbia, Colossus on the Hudson.* New York, 1947.

EDUCATION AND INTELLECTUAL TRENDS

1 COPELAND, Melvin T. *And Mark an Era: The Story of the Harvard Business School.* Cambridge, Mass., 1958.

2 CURTI, Merle, and Vernon CARSTENSEN. *The University of Wisconsin; A History, 1858–1925.* Madison, Wis., 1949.

3 DALEY, John M. *Georgetown University: Origins and Early Years.* Washington, D.C., 1957.

4 DUNBAR, Willis F. *The Michigan Record in Higher Education.* Detroit, 1963.

5 DURKIN, Joseph T. *Georgetown University: The Middle Years (1840–1900).* Washington, D.C., 1963.

6 EARNEST, Ernest Penney. *Academic Procession: An Informal History of the American College, 1636 to 1953.* Indianapolis, 1953.

7 EDDY, Edward Danforth. *Colleges for Our Land and Times: The Land-Grant Idea in American Education.* New York, 1957.

8 ELLIS, John Tracy. *The Formative Years of the Catholic University of America.* Washington, D.C., 1946.

9 ESCHENBACHER, Herman F. *The University of Rhode Island: A History of Land-Grant Education in Rhode Island.* Des Moines, Iowa, 1967.

10 FLEMING, Donald. *Science and Technology in Providence, 1760–1914: An Essay in the History of Brown University in the Metropolitan Community.* Providence, 1952.

11 FORMAN, Sidney. *West Point: A History of the United States Military Academy.* See 47.19.

12 FRENCH, J. C. *A History of the University Founded by Johns Hopkins.* Baltimore, 1946.

13 GANNON, Robert I. *Up to the Present: The Story of Fordham.* Garden City, N.Y., 1967.

14 GATES, Charles M. *The First Century at the University of Washington, 1861–1961.* Seattle, Wash., 1961.

15 GEIGER, Louis G. *University of the Northern Plains: A History of the University of North Dakota, 1883–1958.* Lincoln, Neb., 1958.

16 GLOVER, W. H. *Farm and College: The College of Agriculture of the University of Wisconsin, A History.* Madison, Wis., 1952.

17 GRAY, James. *The University of Minnesota, 1851–1951.* Minneapolis, 1951.

18 HANAWALT, Leslie L. *A Place of Light: The History of Wayne State University.* Detroit, 1968.

19 HAWKINS, Hugh. *Pioneer: A History of the Johns Hopkins University, 1874–1889.* Baltimore, 1960.

20 HOFSTADTER, Richard, and Walter P. METZGER. *The Development of Academic Freedom in the United States.* New York, 1955.

21 HOFSTADTER, Richard, and Wilson SMITH, eds. *American Higher Education, A Documentary History.* 2 vols. Chicago, 1961.

22 HOPKINS, J. F. *The University of Kentucky: Origins and Early Years.* Lexington, Ky., 1951.

EDUCATION AND INTELLECTUAL TRENDS

1. JENCKS, Christopher, and David RIESMAN. *The Academic Revolution.* Garden City, N.Y., 1968.
2. KERSEY, Harry A. Jr. *John Milton Gregory and the University of Illinois.* Urbana, Ill., 1968.
3. Le DUC, Thomas H. *Piety and Intellect at Amherst College, 1865–1912.* New York, 1946.
4. Mc GIFFERT, Michael. *The Higher Learning in Colorado: An Historical Study, 1860–1940.* Boulder, Col., 1964.
5. MARKS, Jeannette. *Life and Letters of Mary Emma Woolley.* See 35.13.
6. MIMS., Edwin. *History of Vanderbilt University.* Nashville, Tenn., 1946.
7. MORISON, Samuel E. *Three Centuries of Harvard, 1636–1936.* Cambridge, Mass., 1936.
8. NASH, Roderick, and Merle CURTI. *Philanthropy in the Shaping of American Higher Education.* See 75.15.
9. NEWCOMER, Mabel. *A Century of Higher Education for American Women.* See 35.16.
10. OLIPHANT, J. Orin. *The Rise of Bucknell University.* Des Moines, Iowa, 1965.
11. PECK, Elizabeth S. *Berea's First Century, 1855–1955.* Lexington, Ky., 1955.
12. PECKHAM, Howard H. *The Making of the University of Michigan, 1817–1967.* Ann Arbor, Mich., 1967.
13. PETERSON, George E. *The New England College in the Age of the University.* Amherst, 1964.
14. PIERSON, George Wilson. *Yale: College and University, 1871–1921.* New Haven, 1952.
15. PIERSON, George Wilson. *Yale: The University College, 1921–1937.* New Haven, 1955.
16. POLLARD, James E. *History of the Ohio State University: The Story of its First Seventy-Five Years, 1873–1948.* Columbus, Ohio, 1952.
17. PORTER, Earl W. *Trinity and Duke, 1892–1924: Foundations of Duke University.* Durham, N.C., 1964.
18. RICHARDSON, Leon Burr. *History of Dartmouth College.* Hanover, N.H., 1932.
19. ROSS, E. D. *Democracy's College: The Land-Grant Movement in the Formative Stage.* Ames, Iowa, 1942.
20. RUDOLPH, Frederick. *The American College and University; A History.* New York, 1962.†
21. RUDY, S. W. *The College of the City of New York.* New York, 1949.
22. SACK, Saul. *History of Higher Education in Pennsylvania.* Harrisburg, Pa., 1963.

1 SCHMIDT, George P. *The Liberal Arts College; A Chapter in American Cultural History.* New Brunswick, N.J., 1957.
2 SELLERS, James B. *History of the University of Alabama.* Tuscaloosa, Ala., 1953.
3 SOLBERG, Winton U. *The University of Illinois, 1867–1894: An Intellectual and Cultural History.* Urbana, Ill., 1968.
4 STORR, Richard J. *The Beginnings of Graduate Education in America.* Chicago, 1953.
5 STORR, Richard J. *Harper's University: The Beginnings. A History of the University of Chicago.* Chicago, 1966.
6 SUTHERLAND, Arthur E. *The Law at Harvard: A History of Ideas and Men, 1817–1967.* Cambridge, Mass., 1967.
7 VEBLEN, Thorstein. *Higher Learning in America.* New York, 1918.†
8 VEYSEY, Lawrence R. *The Emergence of the American University.* Chicago, 1965.
9 VILES, Jonas. *The University of Missouri.* Columbia, Mo., 1939.
10 WILSON, Louis R. *The University of North Carolina, 1900–1930: The Making of a Modern University.* Chapel Hill, 1957.
11 WOODY, Thomas. *A History of Women's Education in the United States.* See 36.7.

D. Libraries, Museums, and Learned Societies

12 BATES, Ralph S. *Scientific Societies in the United States.* 3d Ed. Cambridge, Mass., 1958.
13 DITZION, Sidney. *Arsenals of a Democratic Culture.* Chicago, 1947.
14 DUFFUS, Robert Luther. *Our Starving Libraries.* Boston, 1933.
15 FOX, Daniel M. *Engines of Culture.* See 75.22.
16 GREEN, Samuel Swett. *The Public Library Movement in the United States 1853–1893.* Boston, 1913.
17 HARRIS, Michael H. *A Guide to Research in American Library History.* Metuchen, N.J., 1968.
18 HOSMER, Charles B. Jr. *Presence of the Past: A History of the Preservation Movement in the United States Before Williamsburg.* New York, 1965.
19 KIGER, Joseph C. *American Learned Societies.* Washington, D.C., 1963.
20 KOCH, Theodore Wesley. *A Book of Carnegie Libraries.* White Plains, N.Y., 1917.
21 PACH, Walter. *The Art Museum in America.* New York, 1948.
22 RILEY, Stephen T. *The Massachusetts Historical Society, 1791–1959.* Boston, 1959.

1 THOMPSON, C. Seymour. *Evolution of the American Public Library, 1653–1876.* Washington, D.C., 1952.
2 U.S. Bureau of Education. *Public Libraries in the United States of America: History, Condition, and Management.* Washington, D.C., 1876.
3 U.S. National Museum. *Contributions from the Museum of Science and Technology.* Washington, D.C., 1959.
4 WHITEHILL, Walter M. *Boston Public Library: A Centennial History.* Boston, 1956.
5 WHITEHILL, Walter M. *Independent Historical Societies: An Enquiry into Their Research and Publication Functions and Their Financial Future.* Boston, 1962.
6 WILLIAMSON, William L. *William Frederick Poole and the Modern Library Movement.* New York, 1963.
7 WITTKE, Carl. *The First Fifty Years: The Cleveland Museum of Art, 1916–1966.* See 82.2.

E. Intellectual Trends

8 ADAMS, Henry. *The Education of Henry Adams.* New York, 1918; 1961.†
9 ALEXANDER, Charles C. *Nationalism in American Thought, 1930–1945.* Chicago, 1969.
10 ALLEN, Gay W. *William James: A Biography.* New York, 1967.
11 ARNETT, Willard E. *George Santayana.* Detroit, 1968.
12 BENSON, Leonard G. *National Purpose: Ideology and Ambivalence in America.* See 53.19.
13 BLAU, Joseph. *Men and Movements in American Philosophy.* New York, 1952.
14 BOLLER, Paul F. Jr. *American Thought in Transition: The Impact of Evolutionary Naturalism, 1865–1900.* Chicago, 1969.
15 BOURNE, Randolph. *War and the Intellectuals; Essays, 1915–1919.* Ed. by Carl Resek. New York, 1964.†
16 BROOKS, Van Wyck. *America's Coming of Age.* New York, 1915.
17 CARGILL, Oscar. *Intellectual America; Ideas on the March.* New York, 1968.
18 CASH, Wilbur J. *The Mind of the South.* See 12.10.
19 CHAMBERS, Clarke A. "The Belief in Progress in Twentieth-Century America." *J Hist Ideas,* XIX (1958), 197–224.
20 COHEN, Morris R. *American Thought: A Critical Sketch.* New York, 1954.†
21 COMMAGER, Henry Steele. *The American Mind.* See 78.4.
22 CUNNINGHAM, Horace H. *The Southern Mind Since the Civil War.* See 12.18.
23 CURTI, Merle. *Growth of American Thought.* New York, 1943.

EDUCATION AND INTELLECTUAL TRENDS

1. CURTI, Merle, ed. *American Scholarship in The Twentieth Century.* New York, 1953.
2. DORFMAN, Joseph. *The Economic Mind in American Civilization.* 5 vols. New York, 1959.†
3. DORFMAN, Joseph. *Thorstein Veblen and his America.* New York, 1934.
4. DOWD, Douglas F. *Thorstein Veblen and his America.* Rev. ed. Ithaca, N.Y., 1965.
5. EKIRCH, Arthur A., Jr. *Ideologies and Utopias. The Impact of the New Deal on American Thought.* Chicago, 1969.
6. FLEMING, Donald, and Bernard BAILYN, eds. *The Intellectual Migration: Europe and America, 1930-1960.* See 22.14.
7. GABRIEL, Ralph H. *The Course of American Democratic Thought.* 2d ed., New York, 1956.
8. GREENE, John C. *Objectives and Methods in Intellectual History.* Ames, Ia., 1959.
9. HOFSTADTER, Richard. *Anti-Intellectualism in American Life.* See 58.3.
10. HOFSTADTER, Richard. *The Progressive Historians.* New York, 1968.
11. HOSTADTER, Richard. *Social Darwinism in American Thought 1860-1915.* See 66.4.
12. HOVEY, Richard B. *John Jay Chapman—An American Mind.* New York, 1959.
13. HYMAN, Harold M., and Leonard W. LEVY, eds. *Freedom and Reform: Essays in Honor of Henry Steele Commager.* New York, 1967.
14. JONES, Howard Mumford. *One Great Society: Humane Learning in the United States.* New York, 1959.
15. KENT, Donald P. *The Refugee Intellectual: The Americanization of the Immigrants of 1933-1941.* New York, 1953.
16. KRADITOR, Aileen S. *The Ideas of the Woman Suffrage Movement, 1890-1920.* See 35.9.
17. LERNER, Max. *America as a Civilization: Life and Thought in the United States Today.* See 3.15.
18. MAY, Henry. *The End of American Innocence; A Study of the First Years of Our Own Time, 1912-1917.* See 83.15.
19. MILLER, Perry, ed. *American Thought, Civil War to World War I.* New York, 1954.†
20. NELSON, Benjamin, ed. *Freud and the 20th Century.* Cleveland, 1957.†
21. NOBLE, David W. *The Paradox of Progressive Thought.* See 66.20.
22. NYE, Russel B. *This Almost Chosen People: Essays in the History of American Ideas.* See 78.13.
23. PERRY, Bliss. *The American Mind.* Port Washington, N.Y., 1912.

1 PERRY, Ralph Barton. *The Thought and Character of William James.* Cambridge, Mass., 1954.†
2 PERSONS, Stow. *American Minds. A History of Ideas.* See 78.15.
3 RADER, Benjamin G. *The Academic Mind and Reform: The Influence of Richard T. Ely in American Life.* See 67.1.
4 RESEK, Carl. *Lewis Henry Morgan: American Scholar.* Chicago, 1960.
5 RIESMAN, David. *Thorstein Veblen: A Critical Interpretation.* New York, 1953.
6 ROBINSON, James Harvey. *The New History.* New York, 1965.†
7 SAMUELS, Ernest. *Henry Adams.* 4 vols. Cambridge, Mass., 1948–1964.
8 SANTAYANA, George. *Character and Opinion in the United States.* See 54.21.
9 SCHLESINGER, Arthur M. Jr., and Morton WHITE, eds. *Paths of American Thought.* Boston, 1963.
10 STEVENSON, Elizabeth. *Henry Adams: A Biography.* New York, 1955.†
11 WHITE, Morton G. *Social Thought in America; The Revolt Against Formalism.* New York, 1952.†
12 WISH, Harvey. *Society and Thought in Modern America.* New York, 1952.

XIII. Communications

A. General

13 BODE, Carl. *Mencken.* Carbondale, Ill., 1969.
14 CHAFEE, Zechariah, Jr. *Government and Mass Communications.* Chicago, 1947.
15 ELLIS, Elmer. *Mr. Dooley's America: A Life of Finley Peter Dunne.* New York, 1941.
16 KUEHL, Warren F. *Hamilton Holt: Journalist, Internationalist, Educator.* Gainesville, Fla., 1960.
17 MANCHESTER, William. *Disturber of the Peace; The Life of H. L. Mencken.* New York, 1951.
18 MORRIS, Lloyd R. *Not So Long Ago.* New York, 1949.
19 MORRIS, Lloyd R. *Postscript to Yesterday; America in The Last Fifty Years.* See 3.18.
20 MORRIS, Lloyd R. *William James; The Message of a Modern Mind.* New York, 1950.
21 POE, Clarence Hamilton. *My First 80 Years.* Chapel Hill, 1963.

1 SELDES, Gilbert V. *The New Mass Media; Challenge to Free Society.* Washington, D.C., 1968.

2 STEFFENS, Lincoln. *The Autobiography of Lincoln Steffens.* See 68.4.

3 WHITE, William Allen. *The Autobiography of William Allen White.* New York, 1946.

B. Magazines

4 BAINBRIDGE, John. *Little Wonder; or, The Reader's Digest.* New York, 1946.

5 BLOOMFIELD, Maxwell H. *Alarms and Diversions: The American Mind through American Magazines, 1900–1914.* New York, 1967.

6 CHANDLER, Alfred D. Jr. *Henry Varnum Poor: Business Editor, Analyst, and Reformer.* See 43.10.

7 DOLMETSCH, Carl R. *The Smart Set.* New York, 1966.

8 FILLER, Louis. *Muckrakers: Crusaders for American Liberalism.* See 6.15.

9 GRIMES, Alan P. *The Political Liberalism of the New York Nation, 1865–1932.* Chapel Hill, 1953.†

10 HUMES, D. Joy. *Oswald Garrison Villard, Liberal of the 1920's.* Syracuse, 1960.

11 KOBLER, John. *Luce: His Time, Life and Fortune.* Garden City, N.Y., 1968.

12 LYON, Peter. *Success Story. The Life and Times of S. S. McClure.* New York, 1963.

13 Mc CLURE, S. S. *My Autobiography.* New York, 1914.

14 MOTT, Frank Luther. *A History of American Magazines.* 5 vols. Cambridge, Mass., 1938–1968.

15 O'NEILL, William L., ed. *Echoes of Revolt. The Masses, 1911–1917.* See 68.13.

16 PETERSON, Theodore. *Magazines in the Twentieth Century.* 2d ed. Urbana, Ill., 1964.

17 STERN, Madeline B. *Purple Passage: The Life of Mrs. Frank Leslie.* Norman, Okla., 1953.

18 SWADOS, Harvey. *Years of Conscience—The Muckrakers.* See 7.6.

19 TEBBEL, John William. *George Horace Lorimer and The Saturday Evening Post.* Garden City, N.Y., 1948.

20 VILLARD, Oswald Garrison. *Fighting Years.* New York, 1939.

21 WEINBERG, Arthur M. and Lila. *The Muckrakers.* See 7.7.

22 WOOD, James Playsted. *Magazines in the United States: Their Social and Economic Influence.* New York, 1949.

23 WRESTON, Michael. *Oswald Garrison Villard: Pacifist at War.* Bloomington, 1965.

C. Newspapers

1 CARLSON, Oliver, and Ernest Sutherland BATES. *Hearst, Lord of San Simeon.* New York, 1936.

2 CARTER, Hodding. *Their Words Were Bullets.* Athens, Ga., 1970.

3 CLARK, Thomas D. *The Rural Press and the New South.* See 12.13.

4 CLARK, Thomas D. *The Southern Country Editor.* See 12.14.

5 CONRAD, Will C., and Dale and Kathleen F. WILSON. *The Milwaukee Journal: The First Eighty Years.* Madison, Wis., 1964.

6 EMERY, Edwin. *The Press in America: An Interpretive History Of Journalism.* 2d ed., New York, 1962.

7 JUERGENS, George. *Joseph Pulitzer and the New York World.* Princeton, 1966.

8 KABRE, Sydney. *The Yellow Press and Gilded Age Journalism.* Tallahassee, Fla., 1964.

9 MITCHELL, Joseph. *My Ears are Bent.* New York, 1938.

10 MOTT, Frank Luther. *American Journalism: A History, 1690–1960.* 3d ed., New York, 1962.

11 NIXON, Raymond B. *Henry W. Grady.* New York, 1969.

12 PERKIN, Robert L. *The First Hundred Years: An Informal History of Denver and the Rocky Mountain News.* Garden City, N.Y., 1959.

13 PHELAN, Mary Cortona. *Manton Marble of the New York World.* Washington, D.C., 1957.

14 RAMMELKAMP, Julian S. *Pulitzer's "Post Dispatch", 1878–1883.* Princeton, N.J., 1967.

15 SEITZ, D. C. *Joseph Pulitzer; His Life and Letters.* New York, 1924.

16 STEWART, Kenneth Norman, and John William TEBBEL. *Makers of Modern Journalism.* New York, 1962.

17 STONE, Candace. *Dana and the Sun.* New York, 1938.

18 SWANBERG, W. A. *Citizen Hearst.* New York, 1961.

19 TEBBEL, John William. *An American Dynasty.* New York, 1947.

20 TEBBEL, John William. *The Life and Good Times of William Randolph Hearst.* New York, 1952.

21 WEISBERGER, Bernard A. *The American Newspaperman.* Chicago, 1961.

22 WEISBERGER, Bernard A. *Reporters for the Union.* Boston, 1953.

23 WILCOX, Delos F. "The American Newspaper: A Study of Social Psychology." *Ann Am Acad Pol Soc Sci*, XVI (July, 1900), 56–92.

24 WITTKE, Carl. *The German-Language Press in America.* Lexington, Ky., 1957.

D. Book Publishing

1 CLARK, Aubert J. *The Movement for International Copyright in 19th Century America.* Washington, D.C., 1960.
2 HARPER, J. Henry. *The House of Harper.* New York, 1912.
3 LEHMANN-HAUPT, Hellmut. *The Book in America.* Rev. ed. New York, 1951.
4 MADISON, Charles Allan. *Book Publishing in America.* New York, 1966.
5 MADISON, Charles Allan. *The Owl Among Colophons: Henry Holt as Publisher and Editor.* New York, 1966.
6 MOTT, Frank Luther. *Golden Multitudes.* New York, 1947; 1960.
7 SHEEHAN, Donald. *This Was Publishing: A Chronicle of the Book Trade in the Gilded Age.* Bloomington, 1952.
8 TRYON, Warren S. *Parnassus Corner: A Life of James T. Fields, Publisher to the Victorians.* Boston, 1963.

E. Radio and Television

9 BARNOUW, Erik. *A Tower in Babel: A History of Broadcasting in the United States.* New York, 1966.
10 CANTRIL, Hadley, and Gordon W. ALLPORT. *The Psychology of Radio.* New York, 1941.
11 CHASE, Francis. *Sound and Fury: An Informal History of Broadcasting.* New York, 1942.
12 COLEMAN, Howard W. *Color Television; The Business of Colorcasting.* New York, 1968.
13 LAZARSFELD, Paul F. *The People Look at Radio.* Chapel Hill, 1946.
14 SELDES, Gilbert. *The Great Audience.* New York, 1956.
15 SETTEL, Irving. *A Pictorial History of Radio.* Rev. ed. New York, 1967.

XIV. Science

A. General

16 BARBER, Bernard. *Science and the Social Order.* Rev. ed., New York, 1963.†
17 CONANT, James B. *Modern Science and Modern Man.* New York, 1952.†

1. CONANT, James Bryant. *Science and Common Sense.* New Haven, 1951.†
2. CROWTHER, James Gerald. *Discoveries and Inventions of the 20th Century.* 5th ed. New York, 1966.
3. CROWTHER, James Gerald. *Famous American Men of Science.* New York, 1937.
4. DRUCKER, Peter F. *The New Society: The Anatomy of the Industrial Order.* New York, 1950.†
5. DUPREE, A. Hunter. *Science in the Federal Government: A History of Policies and Activities to 1940.* Cambridge, Mass., 1957.
6. FLEMING, Donald H. *John William Draper and the Religion of Science.* Cambridge, Mass., 1959.
7. GILMAN, William. *Science: USA.* New York, 1965.
8. JAFFE, Bernard. *Men of Science in America.* New York, Rev. ed. 1958.
9. LURIE, Edward. *Louis Agassiz: A Life in Science.* Chicago, 1960.†
10. OPPENHEIMER, J. Robert. *Science and the Common Understanding.* New York, 1954.†
11. PRICE, Don K. *Government and Science: Their Dynamic Relation in American Democracy.* New York, 1962.†
12. U.S. Office of Scientific Research and Development. *Science, the Endless Frontier.* Washington, D.C., 1945. (A Report to the President by Vannevar Bush.)
13. VANCE, Maurice M. *Charles Richard Van Hise: Scientific Progressive.* Madison, Wis., 1960.
14. VAN TASSEL, David D., and Michael G. HALL. *Science and Society in the United States.* Homewood, Ill., 1966.†
15. WHITE, Edward A. *Science and Religion in American Thought.* See 60.6.

B. Health and Medicine

16. ADAMS, George Worthington. *Doctors in Blue: The Medical History of the Union Army in the Civil War.* New York, 1952.†
17. ANDERSON, Oscar E., Jr. *The Health of a Nation: Harvey W. Wiley and the Fight for Pure Food.* Chicago, 1958.
18. BAUR, John E. *The Health Seekers of Southern California, 1870–1900.* San Marino, Calif., 1959.
19. BILLINGS, John Shaw. *Selected Papers of John Shaw Billings.* Chicago, 1965.
20. BLAKE, John B., ed. *Safeguarding the Public: Historical Aspects of Medicinal Drug Control.* Baltimore, 1969.
21. BOATNER, Maxine T. *Voice of the Deaf: A Biography of Edward Miner Gallaudet.* Washington, D.C., 1959.

SCIENCE

1. BONNER, Thomas N. *American Doctors and German Universities: A Chapter in International Intellectual Relations, 1870–1914.* Lincoln, Neb., 1963.

2. BONNER, Thomas N. *The Kansas Doctor: A Century of Pioneering.* Lawrence, Kan., 1959.

3. BONNER, Thomas N. *Medicine in Chicago, 1850–1950: A Chapter in the Social and Scientific Development of a City.* Madison, Wis., 1957.

4. BRIEGER, Gert H. "Sanitary Reform in New York City: Stephen Smith and the Passage of the Metropolitan Health Bill." *Bull Hist Med,* XL (1966), 407–429.

5. BURNHAM, John C. "Psychiatry, Psychology, and the Progressive Movement." *Am Q* XII (1960), 457–465.

6. BURHAM, John C. *Psychoanalysis and American Medicine: 1894–1918; Medicine, Science, and Culture.* New York, 1967.

7. BURROW, James G. *AMA: Voice of American Medicine.* Baltimore, 1963.

8. CARSON, Gerald. *One for a Man, Two for a Horse; A Pictorial History, Grave and Comic, of Patent Medicines.* Garden City, N.Y., 1961.

9. CASSEDY, James H. *Charles V. Chapin and the Public Health Movement.* Cambridge, Mass., 1962.

10. CASSEDY, James H. "Muckraking and Medicine: Samuel Hopkins Adams." *Am Q,* XVI (1964), 85–99.

11. CHESNEY, Alan M. *The Johns Hopkins Hospital and the Johns Hopkins University School of Medicine: A Chronicle.* See 88.16.

12. CLAUSEN, John A., and Robert STRAUS, eds. "Medicine and Society." *Ann Am Acad Pol Soc Sci,* CCCXLVI (March 1963), 1–148.

13. CUNNINGHAM, Horace H. *Doctors in Gray: The Confederate Medical Service.* Baton Rouge, 1958.

14. DAVIS, Audrey W. *Dr. Kelly of Hopkins: Surgeon, Scientist, Christian.* Baltimore, 1959.

15. DOLAN, Edward F. Jr., and H. T. SILVER. *William Crawford Gorgas, Warrior in White.* New York, 1968.

16. DUFFUS, Robert Luther, and L. Emmett HOLT, Jr. *L. Emmett Holt, Pioneer of a Children's Century.* New York, 1940.

17. FLEMING, Donald. *William H. Welch and the Rise of Modern Medicine.* Boston, 1954.

18. FLEXNER, Simon and James T. *William Henry Welch and the Heroic Age of American Medicine.* New York, 1968.†

19. GIBSON, John M. *Physician to the World; The Life of General William C. Gorgas.* Durham, N.C., 1950.

20. GIBSON, John M. *Soldier in White: The Life of General George Miller Sternberg.* Durham, N.C., 1958.

21. GROB, Gerald N. *The State and the Mentally Ill: A History of Worcester State Hospital in Massachusetts, 1830–1920.* Chapel Hill, 1966.

SCIENCE

1. JONES, Billy M. *Health-Seekers in the Southwest, 1817–1900.* Norman, Okla., 1967.

2. JORDAN, Philip D. *The People's Health: A History of Public Health in Minnesota to 1948.* St. Paul, Minn., 1953.

3. KONOLD, Donald E. *A History of American Medical Ethics, 1847–1912.* Madison, Wis., 1962.

4. LERNER, Monroe, and Odin W. ANDERSON. *Health Progress in the United States, 1900–1960: A Report of Health Information Foundation.* Chicago, 1963.

5. Mc CLUGGAGE, Robert W. *A History of the American Dental Association: A Century of Health Service.* Chicago, 1959.

6. Mc NEIL, Donald R. *The Fight for Fluoridation.* New York, 1957.

7. PICKARD, Madge Evelyn, and R. Carlyle BULEY. *The Midwest Pioneer: His Ills, Cures, Cares and Doctors.* New York, 1946.

8. RIDENOUR, Nina. *Mental Health in the United States: A Fifty-Year History.* Cambridge, Mass., 1961.†

9. RIVERS, Thomas Milton. *Tom Rivers: Reflection on a Life in Medicine and Science.* Cambridge, Mass., 1967.

10. ROBERTS, Mary M. *American Nursing: History and Interpretation.* New York, 1954.

11. ROSEN, George. *A History of Public Health.* New York, 1958.

12. ROSENBERG, Charles E. *The Cholera Years: The United States in 1832, 1849, and 1866.* Chicago, 1962.

13. RUSSELL, William Logie. *The New York Hospital: A History of the Psychiatric Service, 1771–1936.* New York, 1945.

14. SCHLESINGER, Edward R. *Health Service for The Child.* New York, 1953.

15. SHAPIRO, Sam, Edward R. SCHLESINGER, and Robert E. L. NESBITT, Jr. *Infant, Prenatal, Maternal, and Childhood Mortality in the United States.* Cambridge, Mass., 1968.

16. SHRYOCK, Richard H. *Medical Licensing in America, 1650–1965.* Baltimore, 1967.

17. SHRYOCK, Richard H. *Medicine in America: Historical Essays.* Baltimore, 1966.

18. SHRYOCK, Richard H. *National Tuberculosis Association, 1904–1954: A Study of the Voluntary Health Movement in the United States.* See 76.10.

19. SNYDER, Charles M. *Dr. Mary Walker: The Little Lady in Pants.* New York, 1962.

20. U.S. Public Health Service. *Medical Care in Transition: Reprints from the American Journal of Public Health, 1949–1966.* 3 vols. Washington, D.C., 1964–1967.

21. WILLIAMS, Ralph C. *The United States Public Health Service, 1798–1950.* Washington, D.C., 1951.

22. WOODFORD, Frank B. and Philip P. MASON. *Harper of Detroit: The Origin and Growth of a Great Metropolitan Hospital.* Detroit, 1964.

1 YOUNG, James Harvey. *The Medical Messiahs: A Social History of Health Quackery in Twentieth-Century America.* Princeton, 1967.

2 YOUNG, James Harvey. *The Toadstool Millionaires: A Social History of Patent Medicines in America Before Federal Regulation.* Princeton, 1961.

C. Physical Sciences

3 BAXTER, James P. *Scientists Against Time.* Cambridge, Mass., 1946.†

4 CALHOUN, Daniel H. *The American Civil Engineer: Origins and Conflict.* Cambridge, Mass., 1960.

5 COLBERT, Monte A. *The Mechanical Engineer in America, 1830–1910: Professional Cultures in Conflict.* Baltimore, 1967.

6 DUPREE, A. Hunter. *Asa Gray, 1810–1888.* Cambridge, Mass., 1959.

7 EMME, Eugene M. *Aeronautics and Astronautics: An American Chronology of Science and Technology in the Exploration of Space, 1915–1960.* Washington, D.C., 1961.

8 HAYNES, William. *American Chemical Industry.* 6 vols. New York, 1945–1954.

9 HEWLETT, Richard G., and Oscar E. ANDERSON, Jr. *The New World, 1936–1946: A History of the United States Atomic Energy Commission.* State College, Pa., 1962.

10 LAPP, Ralph Eugene. *Atoms and People.* New York, 1956.

11 LAPP, Ralph Eugene. *The New Priesthood: The Scientific Elite and The Uses of Power.* New York, 1965.

12 MANNING, Thomas G. *Government in Science: The U.S. Geological Survey, 1867–1894.* Lexington, Ky., 1967.

13 RUKEYSER, Muriel. *Willard Gibbs.* Garden City, N.Y., 1942.

14 WHITNAH, Donald R. *A History of the United States Weather Bureau.* New York, 1961.†

15 WILKINS, Thurman. *Clarence King: A Biography.* New York, 1958.

D. Social and Behavioral Sciences

16 BARITZ, Loren. *The Servants of Power. A History of the Use of Social Science in American Industry.* Middletown, Conn., 1960.†

17 BUCK, Paul H., ed. *Social Sciences at Harvard, 1860–1920; From Inculcation to the Open Mind.* Cambridge, Mass., 1965.

18 CAHNMAN, Werner J., and Alvin BOSKOFF, eds. *Sociology and History: Theory and Research.* New York, 1964.

1. CHALLENGER, Richard D., and Maurice LEE, Jr. "History and The Social Sciences: The Problem of Communications." *Am Hist Rev*, LXI (1955–1956), 331–338.

2. COCHRAN, Thomas, and Richard HOFSTADTER. "History and The Social Sciences." *The Varieties of History from Voltaire to the Present.* Ed. by Fritz Stern. Cleveland and New York, 1956.

3. COX, C. Benjamin, and Byron G. MASSIALAS, eds. *Social Studies in the United States: A Critical Appraisal.* New York, 1967.

4. DEPILLIS, Mario S. "Trends in American Social History and the Possibilities of Behavioral Approaches." *J Soc Hist* I (1967–68), 37–60.

5. GIBSON, John S. *New Frontiers in the Social Studies.* New York, 1967.†

6. HINKLE, Roscoe C. and G. J. *The Development of Modern Sociology: Its Nature and Growth in the United States.* New York, 1954.†

7. LAZARSFELD, Paul et al. *The People's Choice.* New York, 1948.†

8. MAZLISH, Bruce, ed. *Psychoanalysis and History.* Englewood Cliffs, N.J., 1963.

9. MILLS, C. Wright. *The Sociological Imagination.* New York, 1959.†

10. SAVETH, Edward N. *American History and the Social Sciences.* New York, 1964.

11. Social Science Research Council. *Social Sciences in Historical Study: A Report of the Committee on Historiography.* Bulletin 54. New York, 1954.

12. STEIN, Maurice. *The Eclipse of Community: An Interpretation of American Studies.* New York, 1960.†

13. WARNER, William Lloyd. *Democracy in Jonesville.* New York, 1949.†

14. WILLIAMS, Robin M. Jr. *American Society. A Sociological Interpretation.* 2d ed., New York, 1960.

NOTES

INDEX

A—B

Aaron, Daniel, 1.1, 68.19, 69.22, 82.5
Abegglen, James C., 44.20
Abbott, Grace, 37.9, 73.1
Abell, Aaron I., 60.7–8, 61.3
Abrams, Ray A., 58.13
Adamic, Louis, 22.6
Adams, Andy, 42.19
Adams, Ben, 16.14
Adams, Evelyn C., 33.14
Adams, George Worthington, 98.16
Adams, Graham, 48.7
Adams, Henry, 92.8
Adams, James T., 1.2
Adams, Leonard P., 48.8
Adams, Ramon F., 1.3, 42.20–21
Adams, Samuel H., 7.9
Addams, Jane, 6.10, 17.9, 65.1, 75.4
Agee, James, 12.5
Ahearn, Daniel J., Jr., 48.9
Ahlstrom, Sydney E., 61.4
Albright, Raymond W., 61.5
Alexander, Charles C., 57.12, 92.9
Alinsky, Saul D., 48.10, 67.11
Allen, Frederick Lewis, 3.7, 4.2, 7.10–11, 8.16, 43.7
Allen, Gay W., 92.10
Allen, Herman R., 88.3
Allen James B., 16.1
Allen, Ruth A., 48.11
Allport, Gordon W., 97.10
Allsop, Kenneth, 48.12
Alsberg, H. G., 7.12
Altgeld, John P., 65.2
Altmeyer, Arthur J., 73.2
Alvarez, Hernandez, 26.1
Ambler, Charles H., 11.20
Ambrose, Stephen E., 47.13, 88.4
American Historical Association, 1.4–6
American Jewish Periodical Center, 1.7
Amory, Cleveland, 21.7
Ander, Oscar Fritiof, 22.7, 23.14
Andersen, Arlow W., 61.6
Anderson, George L., 14.19
Anderson, Mary, 34.14
Anderson, Odin W., 73.3, 100.4
Anderson, Oscar E., Jr., 39.11, 98.17, 101.9
Anderson, Wilbert L., 41.5
Andrews, Edward Deming, 61.7
Andrews, Frank Emerson, 75.5–7

Andrews, Wayne, 79.4
Angle, Paul M., 53.3
Anshen, Ruth Nanda, 36.8
Anthony, Katherine, 34.15
Arden, G. Everett, 61.8
Arnett, Willard E., 92.11
Aronson, Robert L., 48.8
Arrington, Leonard J., 61.9
Ashburn, Frank D., 87.11
Athearn, Robert G., 14.20, 16.2, 44.22
Atherton, Lewis, 10.18, 42.22
Auerbach, Jerold S., 48.13
Automobile Manufacturers Association, 44.23

Babbidge, Homer D., Jr., 88.5
Bagdikian, Ben H., 72.3
Bailey, Hugh C., 70.1
Bailey, Kenneth K., 61.10
Bailyn, Bernard, 22.14, 93.6
Bainbridge, John, 14.21, 95.4
Baker, Elizabeth F., 34.16, 50.16
Baker, Gladys L., 40.3
Baker, Olin Edwin, 40.4
Baldwin, James, 26.14–15
Baltzell, E. Digby, 21.8, 61.11
Bancroft, Gertrude, 48.14
Barber, Bernard, 97.16
Bardolph, Richard, 32.14
Baritz, Loren, 101.16
Barker, Virgil, 79.5
Barnard, John, 88.6
Barnes, Cass G., 14.22
Barnett, James H., 84.15
Barnouw, Erik, 97.9
Barns, William D., 41.14
Baron, Salo W., 64.1
Barr, A. H., Jr., 79.11
Barrett, Russell H., 56.21
Barry, Colman James, 63.7
Barth, Alan, 56.6
Barth, Gunther, 25.11
Barthelmess, Casey E., 47.20
Bartley, Numan V., 57.1
Bassett, T. D. Seymour, 1.8
Bates, Ernest Sutherland, 96.1
Bates, J. Leonard, 77.12
Bates, Ralph S., 91.12
Baur, John E., 98.18
Baur, John I. H., 79.6, 80.1
Baxter, James P., 101.3
Beals, Carleton, 53.4

INDEX

B

Bean, Walton E., 16.15, 71.6
Beard, Charles A., 3.8, 7.13
Beard, Mary R., 3.8, 7.13
Beaver, R. Pierce, 33.15
Beck, Warren A., 16.3
Becker, Dorothy G., 72.4
Becker, Joseph M., 73.4
Beer, Thomas, 5.11
Beers, Henry P., 1.9
Beirne, Francis F., 17.10
Bell, Daniel, 53.18, 65.3, 68.6, 68.20, 70.17, 88.7
Bell, Howard M., 37.10
Bell, Winifred, 37.11
Bellah, Robert N., 59.11
Bellamy, Edward, 65.4
Bendix, Reinhard, 21.14
Bennett, Lerone, Jr., 30.2–3, 32.15
Bensman, Joseph, 41.13
Benson, Leonard G., 53.19, 92.12
Bentley, George R., 4.5
Berelson, Bernard, 88.8
Berg, Mrs. Harry, 63.19
Bergman, Leola Nelson, 23.15
Berkhofer, Robert F., Jr., 1.10
Berman, Hyman, 49.7
Bernard, Jessie, 37.12
Bernstein, Barton J., 67.12
Bernstein, Irving, 48.15, 50.17
Bernstein, Samuel, 68.21
Berry, Brewton, 33.16, 57.13
Bertelson, David, 12.6
Berthoff, Rowland Tappan, 24.1, 70.18
Berthoff, Warner, 82.6
Bestor, Arthur E., 71.1, 87.12–13
Bettersworth, John K., 12.7
Betts, John R., 85.22
Bier, Jesse, 82.7
Bikle, Lucy Leffingwell, 82.8
Billings, John Shaw, 98.19
Billington, Ray Allen, 13.21, 79.7
Bird, Caroline, 7.14
Birmingham, Stephen, 21.9
Bishop, Morris, 88.9
Blair, Lewis A., 26.16
Blake, John B., 98.20
Blake, Nelson M., 1.11, 3.9, 17.11, 36.9
Blau, Joseph L., 64.1, 92.13
Blaw, Duncan, 21.10
Blaw, Peter Michael, 21.10
Blegen, Theodore C., 23.16, 88.10
Blesh, Rudi, 79.8

Bliss, W. D. P., 1.12
Bloch, Herman D., 32.6–7
Blodgett, Geoffrey, 71.7
Bloomfield, Maxwell H., 95.5
Blum, Albert A., 47.14
Blum, Daniel, 82.9
Blumberg, Dorothy Rose, 34.17
Blume, William Wirt, 88.13
Boardman, Fon W., Jr., 7.15
Boas, George, 78.1
Boatner, Maxine T., 98.21
Boatwright, Mody C., 86.1
Bode, Carl, 94.13
Bogue, Allan G., 11.1, 40.5–6
Bogue, Donald J., 22.3
Bogue, Margaret B., 15.1, 40.7
Boller, Paul F., Jr., 92.14
Bond, Floyd A., 72.5
Bond, Horace M., 31.7–8
Bone, Robert A., 31.9
Bonner, Thomas N., 99.1–3
Boorstin, Daniel J., 3.10, 65.10
Bornet, Vaughn Davis, 73.5
Bourke-White, Margaret, 7.17
Bourne, Randolph, 37.13, 92.15
Bowman, Sylvia E., 65.6
Brace, Charles Loring, 37.14
Braden, Charles S., 58.14–15
Bradford, Gamaliel, 61.12
Bradford, M. E., 67.6
Bradway, John S., 34.18
Braeman, John, 3.11, 7.16, 61.16
Brandeis, Elizabeth, 71.8
Brandfon, Robert L., 12.8–9
Brauer, Jerald C., 61.13
Breck, Allen DuPont, 64.2
Breckinridge, Sophonisba P., 34.19
Bremner, Robert H., 1.1, 65.7, 72.6, 74.3, 75.8–10
Bretall, R. W., 59.9
Brickman, William W., 86.19
Bridges, Hal, 43.8
Brieger, Gert H., 99.4
Briggs, Harold E., 16.16
Bright, Arthur A., 39.12
Brink, William, 30.4
Brissenden, Paul F., 50.18, 67.13
Britt, Albert, 11.2, 41.6
Brittain, Marion Luther, 88.11
Broderick, Francis L., 32.16
Brody, David, 50.19–20, 53.5
Broehl, Wayne G., 50.21
Brogan, D. W., 54.1
Brooks, Robert P., 88.12

110

INDEX

Brooks, Van Wyck, 10.4, 78.2, 79.9, 92.16
Brophy, John, 48.16
Brophy, William A., 33.17
Browder, Earl, 69.1
Brown, A. Theodore, 15.2, 17.20
Brown, Claude, 23.17
Brown, Dee, 4.6, 13.22, 34.20
Brown, E. C., 50.4
Brown, Elizabeth G., 88.13
Brown, Ira V., 60.9
Brown, John M., 83.20
Brown, Mark H., 15.3
Browne, Henry J., 60.9
Bruce, Robert V., 4.7, 48.17, 53.6
Bruno, Frank J., 75.11
Buck, Paul H., 4.8, 101.16
Buck, Solon J., 41.15–16
Bucke, Emory S., 61.14
Budd, Louis J., 65.8, 82.10
Buder, Stanley, 17.12, 43.9
Buley, R. Carlyle, 100.7
Bullock, Henry A., 31.10
Burchard, John, 18.6, 79.10
Burchinal, Lee G., 37.15
Burlingame, Roger, 54.2
Burma, John H., 26.2
Burn, James D., 4.9
Burnham, John C., 76.18, 99.5–6
Burns, W. Haywood, 30.5
Burr, Nelson R., 1.13
Burrow, James G., 46.21, 99.7
Busbey, Katherine, 36.10
Bush-Brown, Albert, 79.10
Butts, Robert Freeman, 58.16, 78.3
Byrne, Frank L., 76.19

Cable, George W., 30.6
Cahill, Holger, 79.11, 85.13
Cahnman, Werner J., 101.17
Caldwell, Erskine, 7.17
Calhoun, Arthur W., 36.11
Calhoun, Daniel H., 101.4
Calista, Donald J., 32.17
Calkins, Raymond, 76.20
Calvert, Monte A., 46.22
Campbell, Christiana M., 41.17
Campbell, John C., 11.21
Cantril, Hadley, 97.10
Capek, Thomas, 25.4
Cargill, Oscar, 92.17
Carleton, Mark T., 74.10

Carlson, Oliver, 96.1
Carlson, Reynold E., 86.2
Carmichael, Stokely, 30.7
Carpenter, John A., 32.18, 47.15
Carr, R. K., 56.7
Carroll, Gordon, 5.6
Carson, Gerald, 46.23, 54.3, 99.8
Carstensen, Vernon, 40.8, 89.2
Carter, Dan T., 55.5
Carter, Everett, 82.11
Carter, Hodding, 96.2
Carter, Paul A., 60.11, 61.15–16
Cartwright, Morse A., 86.20
Cary, Harold W., 88.14
Cash, Wilbur J., 12.10, 92.18
Cassedy, James H., 99.9–10
Catton, William B., 3.16
Caudill, Harry M., 11.22
Caughey, John W., 16.17, 67.14
Cayton, H. R., 27.4
Cerny, George, 41.18
Chafee, Zechariah, Jr., 56.8, 94.14
Chaffin, N. C., 88.15
Challenger, Richard D., 102.1
Chalmers, David Mark, 65.14, 65.9
Chambers, Clarke A., 7.18, 41.19, 71.9, 92.19
Chandler, Alfred D., Jr., 43.10, 95.6
Charles, Searle F., 73.6
Charlesworth, James C., 20.10
Chase, Francis, 97.11
Chase, John W., 9.2
Chase, Stuart, 39.13, 77.13–14
Cheit, Earl F., 43.11
Cherrington, Ernest Hurst, 77.1
Chesney, Alan M., 88.16, 99.11
Chessman, G. Wallace, 88.17
Chester, Edward W., 54.4
Cheyney, E. P., 88.18
Ching, Cyrus S., 48.18
Chiu, Ping, 25.12
Choate, Julian E., Jr., 42.24
Christie, Robert A., 50.22
Christmae, Henry M., 65.2
Churchill, Allen, 6.11
Cicourel, Aaron V., 37.16, 55.6
Clapp, Gordon R., 11.23
Clark, Aubert J., 97.1
Clark, B. H., 82.12
Clark, Elmer T., 58.17
Clark, Ira G., 45.1
Clark, Kenneth Bancroft, 26.18
Clark, Robert D., 61.17

INDEX   C—D

Clark, Thomas D., 12.1, 12.11–16, 47.1, 96.3–4
Clarke, Helen I., 36.12
Clausen, John A., 99.12
Clebsch, William A., 58.18
Clemen, R. A., 43.12
Clement, Travers, 68.5
Cochran, Thomas C., 43.13–15, 45.2, 102.2
Coffin, Tristam P., 85.14
Coffman, Edward M., 47.16
Cogley, John, 58.19
Cohen, Morris R., 92.20
Cohen, Sol, 87.14
Colbert, Monte A., 101.5
Cole, Arthur Charles, 88.19
Cole, Donald B., 22.8
Coleman, Howard W., 97.12
Coleman, James Walter, 53.7
Coles, Robert, 30.8, 37.17
Colman, Gould P., 88.20
Commager, Henry Steele, 21.11, 22.9, 56.9, 65.10, 78.4, 92.21
Commons, John R., 48.19–20
Comstock, Anthony, 37.18
Conant, James Bryant, 87.15, 97.17, 98.1
Condit, Carl W., 79.12–13
Conkin, Paul K., 71.2, 74.4
Conlin, Joseph R., 50.23, 67.15
Conrad, David Eugene, 40.9
Conrad, John P., 74.70
Conrad, Will C., 96.5
Conway, Alan, 24.2
Coon, Horace, 88.21
Cootner, Paul H., 45.3
Copeland, Melvin T., 89.1
Copland, Aaron, 79.14
Core, George, 67.6
Cornell, Robert J., 53.8
Cornely, Paul B., 57.2
Cornwell, Elmer E., Jr., 55.1
Coser Lewis, 69.9
Coulter, E. Merton, 4.10, 12.17, 32.19
Cowing, Cedric B., 38.19, 43.16
Cox, C. Benjamin, 102.3
Coyle, David C., 77.15
Cozens, Frederick W., 86.3
Craig, Tom, 30.21
Cramer, Clarence H., 58.20
Crampton, John A., 42.1
Cremin, L. A., 78.3, 87.16
Cripps, Thomas R., 31.11

Croly, Herbert, 70.2
Cronbach, Abraham, 64.3
Cronon, Edmund David, 32.20
Cross, Robert D., 17.13, 60.12, 63.8
Crowder, Richard, 82.13
Crowther, Bosley, 84.16
Crowther, James Gerald, 98.2–3
Cunningham, Horace H., 12.18, 92.22, 99.13
Cunningham, Raymond J., 61.18
Cunz, Dieter, 24.10
Curran, Francis X., 58.21
Current, Richard N., 39.14
Curti, Merle, 14.1, 54.5, 65.11, 75.12–15, 78.5 86.21, 89.2, 90.8, 92.23, 93.1
Cutlip, Scott M., 75.16

Dabney, Virginius, 77.2
Dahl, Robert A., 17.14
Dakin, Edwin Franden, 61.19
Dale, Edward E., 14.2
Daley, John M., 89.3
Damon, Ethel M., 16.18
Dana, Samuel T., 40.10
Daniels, Jonathan, 7.19
Daniels, Roger, 57.15
David, Henry, 53.9
David, Jay, 27.1
Davidson, Donald, 12.19
Davidson, Martha, 81.5
Davie, M. R., 22.10
Davies, Richard O., 74.5
Davies, Wallace Evan, 47.17, 54.6, 57.16
Davis, Allen F., 34.21, 51.1, 73.7, 75.17
Davis, Allison, 12.20, 27.2, 37.19
Davis, Audrey, 99.14
Davis, Edwin A., 12.21
Davis, Elmer, 56.10
Davis, Moshe, 64.4
Daws, Gavin, 16.19
Day, A. Grove, 16.20
Day, Alice Taylor, 20.11
Day, Lincoln H., 20.11
Dearing, Mary R., 47.18
Debo, Angie, 15.4
DeForest, Robert W., 74.6
Degler, Carl N., 17.15, 35.1
DeGrazia, Alfred, 73.8

INDEX D—F

DeGroot Alfred T., 62.1
Denney, Reuel, 84.17, 86.13
Deppe, Theodore R., 86.2
Depillis, Mario S., 102.4
Derber, Milton, 7.20, 48.20
DeSola, David, 64.5
Destler, Chester McArthur, 65.12, 67.16
Dewey, John, 70.3, 86.22, 87.1
Dewhurst, James F., 9.12
Diamond, Sigmund, 43.17
Dick, Everett, 14.3
Dillon, Richard H., 25.13
Dinnerstein, Leonard, 57.17
Ditzion, Sidney, 36.13, 91.13
Divine, Robert A., 22.11
Doan, Edward, 71.10
Dolan, Edward F., Jr., 99.15
Dollard, John, 12.22, 27.2, 37.19
Dolmetsch, Carl R., 95.7
Donahue, Gilbert E., 3.2, 52.14
Donald, David, 4.21
Donald, H. H., 27.3
Dore, Grazia, 24.15
Dorfman, Joseph, 93.2-3
Dorn, Jacob H., 60.13
Dorson, Richard M., 85.15-16
Douglas, Dorothy, 38.7
Douglas, Marjory S., 13.1
Douglas, Paul H., 38.20, 49.1
Douglas, Frederick, 32.21
Dowd, Douglas F., 65.13, 93.4
Drake, St. Clair, 27.4
Draper, Theodore, 69.2
Dreiser, Theodore, 7.21
Drimmer, Melvin, 28.17
Drinnon, Richard, 67.17
Driver, Harold E., 33.18
Drucker, Peter F., 98.4
Dubofsky, Melvyn, 51.2
DuBois, W. E. B., 27.5-6, 31.12, 33.1, 36.14
Due, John F., 45.22
Duffus, Robert Luther, 12.2, 78.7, 91.14, 99.16
Dufour, Charles L., 13.2
Dulles, Foster Rhea, 30.9, 49.2, 75.18, 86.4
Dunbar, Willis F., 89.4
Duncan, Hugh D., 82.14
Dupree, A. Hunter, 98.5, 101.6
Durkin, Joseph T., 89.5
Dykeman, Wilma, 13.3
Dykstra, Robert R., 14.4, 42.23

Earnest, Ernest Penney, 89.6
Earhart, Mary, 35.2
Eastman, Max, 69.3
Eaton, Clement, 4.11
Eddy, Edward Danfort, 89.7
Eddy, Sherwood, 37.20, 60.14
Edel, Leon, 78.6
Editors of *Art in America*, 79.15
Editors of *Fortune*, 9.3
Edwards, Charles E., 45.4
Egbert, Donald D., 1.8, 68.7
Ekirch, Arthur A., Jr., 70.4, 93.5
Eldredge, H. Wentworth 17.16
Eldridge, Hope T., 20.12
Eliot, Alexander, 79.16
Eliot, Thomas H., 73.9
Elliott, Russell R., 45.5
Ellis, Elmer, 94.15
Ellis, John Tracy, 1.15, 63.9-10, 89.8
Ellison, Ralph, 27.7
Elson, Ruth Miller, 87.17
Emery, Edwin, 96.6
Emme, Eugene M., 45.6, 101.7
Emmet, Boris, 47.2
Engberg, George B., 45.7
Epstein, Abraham, 73.10
Epstein, Melech, 49.3
Erickson, Charlotte, 22.12
Erikson, Erik H., 37.21
Esarey, Logan, 11.3
Eschenbacher, Herman F., 89.9
Essien-Udom, E. U., 30.10
Eubanks, John Evans, 77.3
Evans, Walker, 7.22, 12.5
Ewen, David, 82.15
Ewers, John C., 33.19

Fabos, Julius, 79.17
Fairchild, Henry Pratt, 24.16
Farley, Reynolds, 27.8
Farrell, John C., 65.14
Faulk, Odie B., 16.4
Faulkner, Harold U., 5.12, 6.12-14, 71.11
Felheim, Marvin, 82.16
Fels, Rendigs, 38.21
Felt, Jeremy P., 37.22
Felton, W. R., 15.3
Fermi, Laura, 22.13
Field, Matthew C., 15.5
Filene, Peter G., 69.4
Filler, Louis, 1.17, 6.15, 70.5, 71.12, 95.8

INDEX F—G

Fine, Sidney, 5.13, 49.5, 65.15, 73.11
Fishel, Leslie H., Jr., 27.9
Fishman, Leo, 72.7
Fishwick, Marshall W., 13.4
Fite, David E., 4.12
Fite, Gilbert C., 40.11, 42.2–3
Fitch, James M., 79.18
Fleming, Donald, 22.14. 89.10, 93.6, 98.6, 99.17
Flexner, Abraham, 75.19
Flexner, Eleanor, 35.3
Flexner, James T., 79.19, 99.18
Flexner, Simon, 99.18
Fliegel, Norris E., 81.12
Foerster, Robert Franz, 24.17
Fogelson, Robert M., 17.17
Folks, Homer, 37.23
Folmsbee, Stanley J., 12.3
Foner, Philip S., 51.3
Forcey, Charles, 70.6
Ford, James, 74.7
Forman, Sidney, 47.19, 89.11
Fortune, Editors of, 9.3
Fosdick, Harry E., 61.20
Fosdick, Raymond B., 55.7, 75.20–21
Fox, Daniel M., 65.16, 75.22, 91.15
Franklin, John Hope, 4.13, 27.10, 28.18–19, 30.11, 57.3
Frantz, Joe B., 42.24
Frazier, E. Franklin, 27.11–14, 31.13
Frederic, Harold, 59.1
Freeman, Joseph, 69.5
French, J. C., 89.12
Friedheim, Robert L., 53.10
Friedman, Lawrence M., 74.8
Friedman, Milton, 38.22
Fries, Robert F., 45.8
Frink, Maurice, 43.1, 47.20
Fritz, Henry E., 33.20
Frost, Richard H., 55 8, 67.18
Fuchs, Victor R., 43.18
Fuller, Wayne E., 41.7
Furnas, Joseph C., 7.23, 30.12
Furniss, Norman F., 61.21
Fussell, Edwin, 14.5, 82.17

Gabriel, Ralph H., 93.7
Galbraith, John Kenneth, 8.1, 39.1–2
Galenson, Walter, 51.4
Gallico, Paul, 86.5
Gamio, Manuel, 26.3–4
Gannon, Robert I., 89.13
Gans, Herbert, 17.18, 24.18

Gard, Wayne, 15.6, 43.2, 55.9
Garraty, John A., 5.14, 49.6
Garrison, Winfred Ernest, 59.2, 62.1
Gates, Charles M., 17.1, 89.14
Gates, Paul W., 4.14, 40.12
Gates, Robbins L., 57.4
Gatewood, William B., Jr., 57.18
Gaustad, Edwin Scott, 59.3
Gay, Ruth, 64.6
Geiger, Louis G., 89.15
George, Henry, 65.17
Gerstl, Joel E., 47.7
Gettleman, Marvin E., 9.13
Gibb, George Sweet, 45.9
Gibson, John M., 99.19–20
Gibson, John S., 102.5
Giedion, Siegfried, 39.15
Gilb, Corinne Lathrop, 47.3
Gilbert, Charles E., 73.12
Gilbert, Douglas, 84.18
Gilbert, James Burkhart, 67.19, 82.18
Gilman, William, 98.7
Gilmore, Gladys W., 26.5
Gilmore, N. Ray, 26.5
Ginger, Ray, 5.15–16, 17.19, 57.19, 68.8
Ginzburg, Eli, 49.7
Gitlow, Benjamin, 69.6
Glaab, Charles N., 17.20, 45.10
Glanz, Rudolf, 64.7
Glazer, Nathan, 17.21, 22.15, 64.8, 69.7
Glazer, Sidney, 11.4
Glenn, Norval D., 27.15
Glick, Paul C., 36.15
Glover, W. H., 89.16
Glueck, Sheldon, 55.10
Gohdes, Clarence, 1.18
Goldberg, Arthur J., 51.5
Goldberg, Harvey, 67.20
Goldman, Eric F., 8.2, 9.4, 9.14
Goldmark, Josephine, 35.4
Goldstein, Joseph, 36.16
Goldston, Robert C., 27.16
Gompers, Samuel, 51.6
Goodall, Leonard E., 17.22
Goodman, Paul, 18.1
Goodman, Percival, 18.1
Goodrich, Carter, 39.3, 45.11
Goodrich, Lloyd, 79.20–23, 80.1
Gordon, Milton M., 27.17
Gorer, Geoffrey, 54.7
Gorter, Wytze, 45.12
Gottman, Jean, 18.2

114

G—H INDEX

Gould, Joseph E., 84.19
Gouldner, Alvin W., 53.11
Govorchin, Gerald Gilbert, 25.5
Gowans, Alan, 80.2
Grabill, Wilson H., 20.13
Graham, Otis L., Jr., 8.3
Graham, Patricia Albjerg, 87.18
Graham, Shirley, 33.2
Grant, Joanne, 28.20
Grantham, Dewey W., Jr., 13.5 6
Gray, James, 89.17
Greeley, Andrew M., 63.11
Green, Constance McLaughlin, 12.4, 18.3–5, 28.21
Green, Fletcher M., 74.12
Green, Marguerite, 51.7
Green, Samuel Swett, 91.16
Greenbaum, Fred, 65.18
Greene, John C., 93.8
Greene, Laurence, 8.4
Greene, Lee S., 65.19
Greenleaf, William, 45.13, 75.23
Greenwalt, Emmett A., 71.3
Greer, Thomas H., 65.20, 71.13
Greever, William S., 14.6, 45.14–15
Gregg, Kate L., 15.5
Grier, William H., 27.18
Grinnell, George B., 33.21
Grimes, Alan P., 35.5, 95.9
Griswold, Erwin N., 55.11
Griswold, Wesley S., 45.16
Grob, Gerald N., 49.8, 51.8, 99.21
Grodinsky, Julius, 45.17
Grossman, Jonathan, 51.9
Groves, Ernest R., 35.6, 36.17
Gruenberg, Sidonie M., 35.7
Gruening, Ernest, 16.21
Gunther, John, 9.5
Gurko, Leo, 8.5
Gurr, Ted, 73.8
Gusfield, Joseph R., 77.4
Gutman, Herbert G., 49.9
Guttmann, Allen, 8.6, 70.19

Haber, Samuel, 43.19, 71.14
Hacker, Louis M., 43.20–21
Hagan, William T., 34.1
Haley, Alex, 33.6
Haller, Mark H., 66.1
Hallgren, Mauritz Alfred, 56.11, 67.21
Haltzman, Abraham, 66.2
Hamilton, Charles V., 30.7

Hamer, Phillip M., 2.1
Hanawalt, Leslie L., 89.18
Hand, Learned, 56.12–13
Handlin, Mary, 3.12
Handlin, Oscar, 2.2, 3.12, 18.6, 20.14, 22.16–23.1, 27.19, 64.9
Handy, Robert T., 59.4, 60.15
Hansen, Marcus Lee, 23.2
Hapgood, Hutchins, 72.8
Harbaugh, William H., 6.16
Hareven, Tamara K., 70.7
Harlan, Louis R., 31.14, 33.3, 57.5, 87.19
Harland, Gordon, 59.5
Harper, Fowler V., 36.18
Harper, J. Henry, 97.2
Harrington, Michael, 72.9
Harris, Louis, 30.4
Harris, Michael H., 91.17
Harris, Neil, 5.17
Harris, Sara, 59.6, 74.13
Harrison, Harry P., 84.20
Hart, Henry C., 15.7
Hart, James D., 2.3, 82.19–20
Hart, Jeffrey, 70.20
Hartmann, Edward George, 23.3, 24.3
Hartt, Rollin Lynde, 86.6
Hartz, Louis, 70.8
Harvey, Katherine A., 45.18, 49.10
Hausdorff, Don, 84.21
Hauser, Philip M., 18.7, 20.15
Havighurst, Robert J., 9.6
Hawgood, John A., 14.7
Hawkins, Hugh, 89.19
Haynes, George E., 32.8
Haynes, William, 101.8
Hays, Elinor R., 35.8
Hays, Samuel P., 5.18, 44.1, 77.16
Hayter, Earl W., 40.13
Heady, Earl O., 40.14
Heald, Morrell, 66.3
Healey, James C., 49.11
Heilbron, Bertha L., 15.8
Helgeson, Arlan, 11.5
Helfman, Harold M., 74.14
Heller, James G., 64.10
Helmer, Harriet B., 9.17
Herberg, Will, 59.7
Herndon, James, 31.15
Herreshoff, David, 69.8
Hewitt, Barnard, 82.21
Hewlett, Richard G., 101.9

INDEX H—J

Hickman, Nollie, 45.19
Hicks, Granville, 9.15, 83.1
Hicks, John D., 8.7, 42.8
Hidy, Ralph W., 45.20–21
Hidy, Muriel E., 45.21
Higbee, Edward, 41.8
Higginson, Thomas Wentworth, 4.15, 27.20
Higham, John, 2.4, 23.4, 58.1
Hildebrand, George Herbert, Jr., 45.12
Hill, Frank E., 46.8
Hill, George W., 23.18
Hill, Herbert, 27.21
Hill, Ralph N., 10.5
Hill, Reuben, 36.19
Hilton, George W., 45.22
Hine, Robert V., 71.4
Hinkle, G. J., 102.6
Hinkle, Roscoe C., 102.6
Hirshson, Stanley P., 28.22
Hitchcock, Henry-Russell, 80.3–4
Hitchcock, H. Wiley, 80.5
Hobson, Laura Z., 58.2
Hodge, Frederick Webb, 34.2
Hoffman, Frederick J., 83.2
Hofstadter, Richard, 3.13, 58.3, 66.4, 89.20–21, 93.9–11, 102.2
Hoglund, A. William, 23.17, 42.4
Hohman, Elmo Paul, 49.12
Holbrook, Stewart H., 44.2
Holland, Ada Morehead, 72.23
Holli, Melvin G., 18.8
Hollingshed, August B., 37.24
Hollon, W. Eugene, 15.9–10
Holmes, William F., 74.15
Holt, Glen E., 19.4
Holt, L. Emmett, 99.16
Holt, Rackham, 33.4
Hoover, Edgar M., 18.9
Hopkins, Charles H., 38.1, 60.16–17
Hopkins, J. F., 89.22
Hopkins, J. G. E., 3.14
Horner, Charles F., 84.22
Hosmer, Charles B., Jr., 91.18
Hostetler, John A., 62.2
Hough, Robert L., 66.5
Hovey, Richard B., 93.12
Howard, John Tasker, 80.6–8
Howard, Joseph K., 16.5
Howe, Frederic C., 70.9
Howe, George F., 2.5
Howe, Helen Huntington, 10.6, 54.8
Howe, Henry F., 10.7

Howe, Irving, 51.10, 69.9, 72.12
Howe, Mark Anthony DeWolfe, 55.12, 80.9
Hubbell, Jay B., 83.3
Hudson, Winthrop S., 59.8, 62.3
Hughes, Glen, 83.4
Hughes, Lanston, 29.1–2
Hughes, William H., 33.5
Hull-House, Residents of, 72.10
Hulley, Clarence C., 16.22
Humes, D. Joy, 95.10
Hungerford, Edward, 18.10
Hunker, Henry L., 11.6
Hunt, Paul S., 20.4
Hunter, David R., 18.11
Hunter, Robert, 72.11
Hurst, James Willard, 45.23, 55.13–14
Hutchinson, Edward P., 23.5
Huthmacher, J. Joseph, 10.8, 18.12, 70.10–11
Hyman, Harold M., 58.4, 93.13

Isaacs, Harold R., 27.22
Ise, John, 77.17
Iverson, Robert W., 69.10

Jackson, Joy J., 18.13
Jackson, Kenneth T., 58.5
Jackson, W. Turrentine, 46.1
Jacobs, Jane, 18.14
Jacobs, Lewis, 83.5, 85.1
Jacobs, Norman, 85.2
Jacobs, Paul, 51.11, 67.22
Jacobs Robert D., 84.2
Jacobson, Julius, 32.9, 69.9
Jacobson, Paul, 36.20
Jaffe, Bernard, 98.8
Jaher, Frederic Cople, 66.6
James, Estelle, 51.12
James, Henry, 78.6
James, Ralph, 51.12
James, William, 66.7
Jamison, A. Leland, 1.13, 60.1
Janis, Harriet, 79.8
Janowitz, Morris, 47.21
Jencks, Christopher, 90.1
Jenkins, J. W., 44.3
Jensen, Merrill, 10.1
Jensen, Vernon H., 46.2
Jeuck, John E., 47.2
Johannsen, Albert, 85.3

INDEX

J—L

Johansen, Dorothy O., 17.1
Johnson, Allen, 2.6
Johnson, Arthur M., 46.3–4
Johnson, Charles S., 27.23
Johnson, Donald, 56.14
Johnson, Thomas H., 2.7
Johnston, Alexander, 86.7
Jones, Billy M., 100.1
Jones, Howard Mumford, 2.8, 83.6, 93.14
Jones, Maldwyn, A., 23.6
Jones, Robert Huhn, 6.4
Jones, Thomas C., 9.17
Jordan, Phillip D., 11.7, 100.2
Josephson, Matthew, 39.16, 44.4
Joughin, George Louis, 56.15
Judah, Charles, 5.4
Juergens, George, 96.7

Kabre, Sydney, 96.8
Kadushin, Alfred, 38.2
Kandel, Isaac L., 87.2
Kane, Lucile M., 18.15
Kaplan, Francis B., 35.15
Kaplan, Justin, 83.7
Kaplan, Louis, 2.9
Katz, Jay, 36.16
Katz, William L., 29.3
Kazin, Alfred, 83.8
Keener, Orrin L., 42.5
Kegley, Charles W., 59.9
Keith-Lucas, Alan, 38.3
Keller, Suzanne, 21.12
Kellogg, Charles Flint, 29.4
Kellogg, Paul U., 18.16
Kelly, Fred C., 39.17
Kelly, Lawrence C., 34.3
Kempton, Murray, 69.11
Kennedy, E. D., 46.5
Kent, Donald P., 93.15
Keppel, Frederick Paul, 78.7
Kerr, K. Austin, 46.6
Kersey, Harry A., Jr., 90.2
Kiger, Joseph Charles, 76.1, 91.19
King, Judson, 77.18
King, Martin Luther, 30.13
Kinne, Wisner P., 83.9
Kinsey, A. C, 36.21–22
Kinzer, Donald L., 58.6
Kipnis, Ira, 68.9
Kirk, Russell, 70.21–22
Kirkland, Edward C., 10.9, 44.5–6
Kirwan, Albert D., 12.16

Kisch, Guido, 64.11
Kittridge Henry C., 10.10
Kleppner, Paul J., 55.2
Knight, Arthur, 85.17
Knight, E. W., 87.3
Knowlton, Evelyn H., 45.9
Knox, Israel, 64.12
Knuth, Priscilla, 17.8
Kobler, John, 95.11
Koch, Theodore Wesley, 91.20
Kolehmainen, John I., 23.18
Kolko, Gabriel, 21.13, 44.7
Kolodin, Irving, 80.10
Konnyu, Leslie, 25.6
Konold, Donald E., 100.3
Konvitz, Milton R., 56.16–17
Koren, John, 77.5
Kornwolf, James D., 80.11
Kouwenhoven, John A., 18.17, 78.8, 80.12
Kraditor, Aileen S., 35.9, 93.16
Kramer, Frank R., 85.18
Kramer, Judith R., 64.13
Krech, H.S., 35.7
Kristol, Irving 88.7
Krislov, Samuel, 32.10
Krout, John A., 86.8
Krug, Edward Augustus, 87.20
Kuehl, Warren B., 2.10
Kuehl, Warren F., 2.10, 94.16
Kung, S. W., 25.14
Kuznets, Simon, 22.4

Lahne, Herbert J., 49.13
Lahue, Kalton C., 83.10
Laidler, Harry Wellington, 49.14, 68.10
Lambert, Richard D., 59.10
Lampard, Eric E., 40.15
Landau, Saul, 67.22
Lander, Ernest M., 13.7
Landon, Fred, 11.8
Lane, Robert E., 55.3
Lane, Roger, 18.18, 55.15
Lange, Dorothea, 8.8
Langsam, Miriam Z., 38.4
Lankford, John, 76.2
Lapp, Ralph Eugene, 101.10–11
Larkin, O. W., 80.13
Larner, Jeremy, 72.12
Larrabee, Eric, 84.17
Larson, Henrietta M., 44.8–9
Larson, Taft A., 16.6

INDEX   L—M

Lasch, Christopher, 66.8–9, 67.23
Laski, Harold J., 66.10
Lasslett, John, 49.15
Latham, Earl, 69.12
Lavender, David, 14.8, 15.11
Layer, Robert G., 49.16
Lazarsfeld, Paul F., 97.13, 102.7
Learsi, Rufus, 64.14
Lebhar, Godfrey M., 47.4
LeDuc, Thomas H., 90.3
Lee, Everett S., 20.16
Lee, Joseph, 76.3
Lee, Maurice, Jr., 101.18
Lee, Rose Hum, 25.15
Leech, Margaret, 5.19
Lefler, Hugh T., 13.8
Lehmann-Haupt, Hellmut, 97.3
Leiby, James, 49.17, 73.13
Leighton, Isabel, 8.9
Leiter, Robert D., 51.13–14
Lens, Sidney, 58.7, 67.24, 68.11, 72.13
Leonard, Neil, 80.14
Lerner, Max, 3.15, 54.9, 55.16, 78.9, 93.17
Lerner, Munroe, 100.4
Lescohier, Don D., 49.18
Lester, Richard A., 51.15
Leuchtenburg, William E., 6.17, 8.10
Levasseur, Emile, 49.19
Leventman, Seymour, 64.13
Levine, Daniel, 66.11
Levy, Leonard W., 93.13
Levy, Lester S., 80.15
Lewis, Anthony, 9.16
Lewis, Oscar, 26.6
Leyburn, James G., 24.4
Lifton, Robert Jay, 35.10
Lilienthal David, 70.12
Lillard, Richard G., 2.11, 16.7
Lincoln, C. Eric, 30.14
Lind, Andrew W., 25.16
Lindley, Betty, 38.5
Lindley, Ernest K., 38.5
Lindner, Robert M., 74.16
Lindsey, Almont, 53.12
Lingelbach, William E., 2.12
Link, Arthur S., 3.16, 6.18
Lipset, Seymour Martin, 21.14
Litwack, Leon, 51.16
Lively, Robert A., 39.4
Livermore, Mary A., 36.6
Lloyd, Caroline Augusta, 66.12
Lloyd, Henry Demarest, 66.13

Locke, Alain, 31.17
Loe, Kelly, 72.15
Logan, Frenise A , 29 5
Logan, Rayford W., 27.24, 29.6
Lomax, John A., 80.16
Lomax, Louis E., 30.15
Long, Clarence D., 49.20–21
Lorant, Stefan, 18.19
Lord, Eliot, 46.7
Lord, Walter 6.19
Lorwin, Lewis L., 38.6, 51.17
Lowe, Jeanne R., 18.20
Lubove, Roy, 6.20–21, 73.14, 74.9, 76.4
Lucas, Henry S., 24.11
Ludwig, Richard M., 2.8, 3.1
Luebke, Frederick C., 15.12
Lumpkin, Katherine, 38.7
Lundberg, Emma Octavia, 38.8
Lurie, Edward, 98.9
Lutz, Alma, 35.11
Lynd, Helen M., 20.17, 54.10–11
Lynd, Robert S., 20.17, 54.10–11
Lynes, Russell, 78.10
Lynn, Kenneth S., 54.12, 85.4
Lyon, Peter, 95.12
Lyons, Eugene, 69.13

McAvoy, Thomas T., 63.12–14
McCallum, Frances T., 43.3
McCallum, Henry D., 43.3
McCarthy, Mary, 63.15
McClintock, Inez, 86.9
McClintock, Marshall, 86.9
McCluggage, Robert W., 100.5
McClure, S. S., 95.13
McCluskey, Neil G., 87.4–5
McCoubrey, John W., 2.13, 80.17
McDermott, John F., 15.5
MacDonald, Dwight, 85.5
McDonald, Forest, 44.10–11
McDonald, William F., 78.11, 83.11
McEntire, Davis, 49.22
McFarland, Gerald W., 71.15
McGeary, Martin Nelson, 77.19
McGiffert, Michael, 54.13, 90.4
McGill, Ralph, 13.9
McGovern, James R., 35.12
McGraw, J. J., 86.10
McKelvey, Blake, 18.21–23, 74.17
MacLean, Janet R., 86.2
MacLeish, Archibald, 8.11
McLoughlin, William G., Jr., 59.11, 62.4–6

M INDEX

McMaster, John B., 56.18
MacMullen, Jerry, 17.2
McMurry, Donald L., 53.13
McNeil, Donald R., 100.6
McPherson, James M., 29.7–8
McReynolds, Edwin C., 15.13–14
McWilliams, Carey, 17.3, 25.17, 26.7, 40.16
Madison, Charles Allan, 51.18, 66.14–15, 70.13, 97.4–5
Makdisi, Nadim, 59.12
Malcolm X, 33.6
Malin, James C., 15.15, 40.17, 43.4
Malone, Dumas, 2.6
Man, Alton P., Jr., 50.1
Manchester, William, 94.17
Mandelbaum, Seymour J., 19.1
Mangold, George B., 38.9
Mann, Arthur, 5.20
Manning, Thomas G., 101.12
Manwaring, David R., 59.13
Marcus, Jacob R., 63.19
Marks, Jeannette, 35.13, 90.5
Marsh, George Perkins, 77.20
Marshall, Louis, 55.17
Marshall, F. Ray, 13.10, 32.11, 50.2
Martin, Edgar W., 4.16
Marty, Martin E., 59.14
Marx, Leo, 19.2, 66.16
Mason, Alpheus T., 55.18–19
Massey, Mary Elizabeth, 4.17–18, 35.14
Massiales, Byron G., 102.3
Mathews, Basil, 33.7
Mathews, Jane DeHart, 83.12
Matthews, William, 48.1
Matthiessen, F. O., 83.13–14
Mattfeld, Julius, 80.18
Mauldin, Bill, 9.7
May, George S., 11.9
May, Henry F., 8.12, 60.18, 83.15, 93.18
Mayer, Grace M., 19.3
Mayer, Harold M., 19.4
Maynard, Theodore, 63.16
Mayo, Elton, 39.5
Mazlish, Bruce, 102.8
Mead, Margaret, 35.15, 38.10, 54.14
Mead, Sidney, 59.15
Mears, E. G., 25.18
Mecklin, John Moffatt, 58.8
Meeks, Carroll L. V., 80.19
Meier, August, 29.9, 31.18, 66.17

Mellquist, Jerome, 80.20
Meltzer, Milton, 29.2
Mencher, Samuel, 73.15
Mencken, H. L., 83.16
Mendelowitz, Daniel M., 80.21
Meriam, Lewis, 34.4
Mermelstein, David, 9.13
Merrill, Francis E., 9.8
Metz, Charles, 77.6
Metz, Harold, 50.3
Metzger, Walter P., 89.20
Meyer, Donald B., 62.7–8
Meyer, Roy W., 34.5, 83.17
Miller, Elizabeth W., 2.14, 27.25, 29.10
Miller, Herman P., 72.14
Miller, Nyle H., 15.16
Miller, Perry, 93.19
Miller, Robert Moats, 31.19, 60.19
Miller, William, 44.12–13
Miller, William D., 19.5
Miller, William L., 19.6
Miller, Zane L., 19.7
Millis, Harry A., 50.4
Mills, C. Wright, 21.15–16, 102.9
Mims, Edwin, 90.6
Minehan, Thomas, 38.11
Mitchell, Broadus, 8.13, 39.18
Mitchell, George S., 39.18, 51.19
Mitchell, Joseph, 96.9
Mizener, Arthur, 83.18
Moberg, Wilhelm, 23.19
Moley, Raymond, Jr., 48.2
Moody, Ralph, 14.9
Mooney, Hughson F., 80.22
Moore, Joan W., 26.8
Moore, John Hammond, 5.3, 30.20
Moore, Wilbert E., 50.5
Morgan, Arthur E., 66.18
Morgan, Dale L., 14.10, 16.8
Morgan, Edmund M., 56.15
Morgan, H. Gerthon, 9.6
Morgan, H. Wayne, 5.21, 6.1, 49.9, 68.12
Morison, Elting E., 3.17, 39.19, 54.15, 78.12
Morison, Samuel E., 90.7
Morris, James O., 51.20
Morris, Lloyd R., 3.18, 83.19, 94.18–20
Morris, Richard B., 2.15, 55.20
Morris, Wright, 8.14
Mortensen, A. Russell, 62.9
Moses, Montrose J., 83.20

INDEX   M—P

Mott, Frank Luther, 95.14, 96.10, 97.6
Mowry, George E., 7.1, 8.15, 19.8, 71.16
Moynihan, Daniel P., 17.21, 22.15
Mueller, John H., 80.23
Muir, William K., Jr., 59.16, 87.6
Mulder, William, 23.20, 62.9–10
Mumford, Lewis, 6.2, 19.9, 81.1–2
Murdock, G. P., 20.18
Murphy, Paul L., 58.9
Murray, Robert K., 7.2, 58.10
Murrell, William, 85.6
Muse, Benjamin, 29.11, 57.6
Myrdal, Gunnar, 28.1

Napolska, Sister Mary Remigia, O.S.F., 25.7
Nash, Roderick, 54.16, 75.15, 90.8
National Research Council et al., 2.16
Neely, Wayne C., 41.9
Nelson, Benjamin, 93.20
Nelson, James, 51.21
Nesbitt, Robert E. L. Jr., 100.15
Neu, Irene D., 46.17
Neuberger, Richard L., 72.15
Neufeld, Maurice F., 2.18, 51.22
Nevins, Allan, 2.19, 4.19–20, 19.10, 44.14, 46.8, 76.5
New York Times, 9.16
Newby, I. A., 30.16, 57.7, 66.19
Newcomer, Mabel, 35.16, 44.15, 90.9
Newfield, Jack, 68.1
Newell, Barbara Warne, 51.23
Newsome, Albert R., 13.8
Nichols, Roy F., 59.17
Nicoll, Bruce H., 15.17
Niebuhr, Reinhold H., 62.11
Niebuhr, Richard H., 59.18–19
Nietz, John A., 83.21
Nixon, Raymond B., 96.11
Noble, David W., 66.20, 93.21
Noble, Stuart G., 87.7
Nolen, Claude H., 30.17
Nowell, Elizabeth, 83.22
North, Douglass C., 39.6
Nute, Grace L., 11.10
Nye, Russel B., 78.13, 93.22

O'Brien, David J., 60.20
O'Dea, Thomas F., 62.12
O'Neill, William L., 10.2, 36.23, 68.13, 95.15
Oehler, Chester M., 34.6
Ogburn, William F., 9.9
Okun, Bernard, 20.19
Oliver, J. W., 39.20
Oliphant, J. Orin, 90.10
Olmstead, Clifton E., 59.20
Olson, James C., 15.18
Oppenheimer, J. Robert, 98.10
Orr, Oliver H., Jr., 87.21
Osofsky, Gilbert, 28.2, 30.18, 31.20
Osterweis, Rollin G., 19.11
Ostrander, Gilman M., 16.9, 77.7
Ottley, Roi, 29.12
Overmyer, Grace, 78.14, 81.3
Overton, Richard C., 46.9
Ovington, Mary White, 28.3

Pach, Walter, 91.21
Packard, Vance O., 47.5
Paden, Irene D., 14.11
Parker, Franklin, 76.6
Parsons, Talcott, 26.18
Patterson, Frederick D., 33.5
Paul, Arnold M., 55.21
Paulson, Ross E., 66.21
Peade, Jane H., 28.4
Pease, Otis, 47.6
Pease, Theodore C., 11.11
Pease, William H., 28.4
Peck, Elizabeth S., 90.11
Peck, Mary Gray, 35.17
Peckham, Howard H., 90.12
Peel, Robert, 62.13
Pelling, Henry, 51.24, 68.14
Penick, James L., 77.21
Perkin, Robert L., 96.12
Perlman, Mark, 52.1–2
Perlman, Selig, 52.3–4
Perrucci, Robert, 47.7
Perry, Bliss, 93.23
Perry, Louis B., 52.5
Perry, Ralph Barton, 94.1
Perry, Richard S., 52.5
Persons, Stow, 1.8, 68.7, 78.15, 94.2
Petersen, William, 21.17, 54.17
Peterson, George E., 90.13
Peterson, Theodore, 95.16
Phelan, Mary Cortona, 96.13
Pickard, Madge Evelyn, 100.7
Pickering, Ernest, 81.4
Pierce, Arthur D., 10.13

INDEX

P–R

Pierce, Bessie L., 19.12
Pierson, George Wilson, 90.14–15
Pierson, William H., Jr., 81.5
Pinchot, Gifford, 77.22
Pitt, Leonard, 26.9
Plaut, W. Gunther, 64.15–16
Plimpton, George, 86.11
Pochmann, Henry A., 78.16
Poe, Clarence Hamilton, 41.10, 94.21
Polenberg, Richard, 9.10
Pollack, Norman, 66.22
Pollard, James E., 90.16
Pomeroy, Earl, 14.12, 17.4
Pool, Tamar, 64.5
Porter, Earl W., 90.17
Potter, David M., 35.18, 54.18
Potwin, Marjorie A., 13.11, 50.6
Pound, Arthur, 11.12
Pound, Louise, 85.19
Powderly, Terence V., 52.6
Powell, John Wesley, 16.10
Powell, Lyman Pierson, 62.14
Pratt, Richard Henry, 34.7
Presbrey, Frank S., 44.16
President's Research Committee, 4.1
Preston, William, Jr., 56.19, 58.11
Prettyman, W. S., 15.19
Price, Don K., 98.11
Prothro, James W., 44.17, 66.23
Pumphrey, Muriel W., 76.7
Pumphrey, Ralph E., 76.7
Puttkammer, Charles W., 33.8

Quaife, Milo M., 11.13
Qualey, Carleton C., 23.21
Quarles, Benjamin, 27.9, 33.9
Quinn, Arthur H., 83.23
Quint, Bernard, 9.5
Quint, Howard H., 13.12, 28.5, 68.15

Raaen, Aagot, 23.22
Radano, Gene, 56.1
Rader, Benjamin G., 67.1, 94.3
Rae, John B., 46.10
Rammelkamp, Julian S., 96.14
Randall, Edwin T., 74.18
Randall, James G., 4.21
Randel, William Pierce, 58.12
Range, Willard, 40.18
Rainwater, Lee, 28.6, 37.1
Ratner, Sidney, 39.7
Rauschenbusch, Walter, 60.21

Rayback, Joseph G., 52.7
Record, Wilson, 28.7–8, 69.14–15
Redding, Saunders, 29.13
Redlich, Fritz, 86.12
Reed, H. H., 19.24
Reed, Walt, 81.6
Rees, Albert, 50.7
Reid, Whitelaw, 5.1
Reissman, Leonard, 21.18
Renshaw, Patrick, 52.8
Reps, John W., 19.13
Resek, Carl, 94.4
Rezneck, Samuel, 5.2, 6.3
Reznikoff, Charles, 94.4
Rice, Charles Scott, 62.15
Rich, Louise D., 10.11
Richardson, Edgar P., 81.7
Richardson, Leon Burr, 90.18
Richardson, Reed C., 52.9
Richmond, Rebecca, 84.7
Rickard, T. A., 46.11
Rickey, Don, Jr., 48.3
Rickover, Hyman G., 87.8
Ridenour, Nina, 100.8
Rideout, Walter B., 68.2, 83.24
Riegel, Robert E., 35.19
Riesman, David, 54.19, 86.13, 90.1, 94.5
Riis, Jacob A., 19.14, 23.7, 72.16–18
Riker, William H., 48.4
Riley, Stephen T., 91.22
Rischin, Moses, 50.8, 54.20, 64.17–18
Rister, Carl C., 15.20
Rivers, Thomas Milton, 100.9
Roberts, Mary M., 100.10
Roberts, Peter, 24.19
Robinson, Cecil, 26.10
Robinson, Elwyn B., 15.21
Robinson, Florett, 3.14
Robinson, James Harvey, 94.6
Robsjohn-Gibbings, Terence Harold, 81.8
Rodman, Selden, 81.9–10
Rogers, Agnes, 4.2, 8.16, 35.20
Rolle, Andrew F., 17.5
Rolt, Lionel T., 39.21
Romasco, Albert U., 8.17
Roper, Elmo B., 55.4
Rose, Arnold M., 28.9, 29.14
Rose, Barbara, 81.11
Rose, Willie Lee, 29.15
Roseboom, Eugene H., 11.14–15
Rosemzweig, Robert M., 88.5
Rosen, George, 100.11

INDEX R—S

Rosenberg, Bernard, 81.12, 85.8
Rosenberg, Charles E., 100.12
Ross, E. D., 90.19
Rossiter, Clinton, 69.16, 70.23
Rosskam, Edwin, 29.23
Rourke, Constance, 84.1
Roy, Ralph Lord, 59.22, 69.17
Rubin, Louis D., Jr., 31.21, 84.2
Ruchames, Louis, 32.12
Rudolph, Frederick, 90.20
Rudwick, Elliott M., 29.9, 30.19, 33.10
Rudy, S. W., 90.21
Rukeyser, Muriel, 101.12
Rumble, Wilfred E., Jr., 56.2
Russ, William A., Jr., 17.6
Russell Sage Foundation, 76.8
Russell, William Logie, 100.13
Ryan, John A., 60.22

Sablosky, Irving, 81.13
Sack, Saul, 90.22
Saloutos, Theodore, 25.1–2, 42.6–8
Samuels, Ernest, 94.7
Sandburg, Carl, 84.3
Sandoz, Mari, 15.22, 34.8, 43.5
Santayana, George, 54.21, 94.8
Santmyer, Helen H., 11.16
Saposs, David Joseph, 52.10–11, 69.18–19
Sappington, Roger E., 61.1
Sarratt, Reed, 57.8
Savage, Howard J., 76.9
Saveth, Edward N., 37.2, 102.10
Scammon, Richard M., 21.6
Schafer, Joseph, 41.11
Scheiner, Seth M., 29.16
Schell, Herbert S., 15.23
Schickel, Richard, 84.4
Schlabach, Theron F., 73.16
Schlebecker, John T., 42.9, 43.6
Schlesinger, Arthur M., 2.22, 19.15, 37.3, 54.22, 67.2
Schlesinger, Arthur M., Jr., 8.18, 70.14, 94.9
Schlesinger, Edward R., 100.14–15
Schmidt, George P., 91.1
Schmitt, Peter J., 19.16
Schneider, Herbert Wallace, 59.23
Schneider, Louis, 59.24
Schnier, Jacques, 81.14
Schnore, Leo F., 18.7
Schoener, Allon, 23.8

Schorer, Mark, 84.5
Schreiber, William I., 62.16
Schrier, Arnold, 24.5
Schriftgiesser, Karl, 8.19
Schuller, Gunther, 81.15
Schuyler, Montgomery, 81.16
Schwartz, Anna J., 38.22
Schwartz, Harold, 71.17
Schwartz, Louis B., 74.19
Schwartz, Mildred A., 47.8
Schweppe, Emma, 42.12
Scott, Anne Firor, 35.21
Scott, John A., 81.17
Scott, Meliero G., 17.7
Scott, Roy V., 42.10
Seabrook, Isaac D., 5.3, 30.20
Sears, Roebuck and Co., 47.9
Seidman, Joel, 52.13
Seitz, D. C., 96.15
Seldes, Gilbert V., 8.20, 85.9, 95.1, 97.14
Seligman, Ben B., 72.19
Sellers, James B., 77.8, 91.2
Sennett Richard, 19.23
Servin, Manuel P., 26.11
Settel, Irving, 97.15
Seward, G. F., 25.19
Sexton, Patricia C., 26.12
Seymour, Harold, 86.14
Shannon, David A., 6.6, 8.21, 68.16, 69.20
Shannon, Fred A., 6.4, 40.19, 41.12, 42.11
Shannon, William, 24.6
Shapiro, Sam, 100.15
Shaplen, Robert, 62.17
Sharlin, Harold T., 39.22
Sharp, Paul F., 14.13
Sheehan, Donald, 97.7
Sheldon, Henry D., 21.1
Shenk, John B., 62.15
Shepperson, Wilbur S., 24.7
Sherman, C. Bezalal, 64.19
Sherman, Richard B., 71.18
Shideler, J. H., 42.12
Shields, Currin V., 63.17
Shogan, Robert, 30.21
Shover, John L., 42.13–14
Shryock, Richard H., 76.10, 100.16–18
Shugg, R. W., 13.13
Siegfried, Andre, 78.17
Sills, David L., 76.11
Silver, H. T., 99.15

122

INDEX

S—T

Silver, James W., 30.22
Simkins, Francis B., 13.14, 42.15
Simon, Rita J., 8.22, 69.1
Simons, A. M., 67.3
Simpson, George E., 34.9
Sinclair, Andrew, 35.22–23, 77.9
Sinclair, Upton Beall, 72.20
Sirjamaki, John, 37.4
Sitterson, J. Carlyle, 40.20
Sizer, Theodore R., 87.22
Sklare, Marshall, 64.20
Sloan, John, 81.18
Slosson, Preston W., 7.3
Smedes, Susan D., 13.15
Smith, Bob, 57.9
Smith Duane A , 46.12
Smith, George W., 5.4
Smith Gibbs M., 68.3
Smith, Henry L., 46.13
Smith, Henry Nash, 85.10
Smith, James Ward, 1.13, 60.1
Smith, Page, 19.17
Smith, Robert, 86.15
Smith, Robert W., 53.14
Smith, Timothy Lynn, 22.5, 23.9, 28.10, 62.18
Smith, Wilson, 89.21
Smuts, Robert W., 36.1
Snyder, Charles M., 100.19
Social Science Research Council, 102.11
Solberg, Winton U., 91.3
Sollid, Roberta Beed, 36.2
Solomon, Barbara Miller, 10.12, 23.10, 64.21
Sorenson, Virginia, 62.19
Souders, David Aaron, 25.8
Soule, George, 7.4, 8.23, 39.8
Spahr, Charles B., 50.9
Spain, Rufus B., 62.20
Spargo, John, 38.12
Spear, Allan H., 28.11
Spence, Clzrk C., 46.14
Spencer, Samuel R., Jr., 33.11
Spiller, Robert E., 3.1, 78.18–19, 84.17
Sprague, Marshall, 46.15
Stampp, Kenneth M., 5.5
Starkey, Marion L., 62.21
Starr, Isidore, 30.11
Stearns, Harold, 8.24, 78.20, 79.1
Stearns, Marshall W., 81.19
Steckmesser, Kent Ladd, 85.20
Steeples, Douglas W., 6.5

Steffens, Lincoln, 68.4, 95.2
Stegner, Wallace, 16.11–12
Stein, Maurice, 102.12
Stember, Charles Herbert, 64.22
Stephenson, George M., 23.11
Stern, Fritz, 102.1
Stern, Madeline B., 36.3, 95.17
Sternsher, Bernard, 29.17
Stevenson, Elizabeth, 94.10
Stewart, George R., 10.3
Stewart, Kenneth Norman, 96.16
Stigler, George J., 47.10
Still, Bayrd, 19.18–19
Stouffer, Samuel A., 48.5, 56.20
Stockwell, Edward G., 21.2
Stokely, James, 13.3
Stone, Candace, 96.17
Storr, Richard J., 91.4–5
Stouffer, Samuel Andrew, 37.5, 48.5, 56.20
Stover, J. F., 46.16
Straus, Robert, 99.12
Strayer, Martha, 36.4
Strecker, Edward Adam, 37.6
Street, James H., 39.23
Stroud, Gene S., 3.2, 52.14
Stroup, Herbert Hewitt, 62.22
Sullivan, Louis H., 81.20
Sullivan, Mark, 7.5
Summers, Festus P., 11.20
Sung, Betty Lee, 25.20
Sutherland, Arthur E., 91.6
Sutton, Francis X., 44.18
Swados, Harvey, 7.6, 50.10, 95.18
Swain, Donald C., 77.23
Swanberg, W. A., 96.18
Sweeney, David F., 63.18
Sweet, William Warren, 60.2, 62.23
Swint, Henry L., 31.22, 32.1
Symes, Lillian, 68.5
Syrett, Harold C., 19.20

Taeuber, Alma F., 28.12, 57.10
Taeuber, Conrad, 21.3
Taeuber, Irene B., 21.3
Taeuber, Karl E., 28.12, 57.10
Taft, Philip, 52.15–18
Taft, Robert, 14.14, 81.21
Tager, Jack, 19.21, 72.1
Tarbell, Ida, M., 44.19
Tatum, George B., 19.22
Taylor, Carl C., 42.16
Taylor, Deems, 85.11
Taylor, George R., 46.17

INDEX T—W

Taylor, P. S., 8.8
Tcherikower, E., 50.11
Tebbel, John William, 21.19, 95.19, 96.16, 96.19–20
Teller, Judd L., 64.23
Thernstrom, Stephan, 19.23, 21.20
Thomas, Dorothy Swaine, 20.12
Thomas, Helen S., 56.3
Thomas, W. I., 25.9
Thompson, C. Seymour, 92.1
Thompson, Lawrence S., 13.16
Thomson, Virgil, 81.22
Thornbrough, Emma Lou, 31.1
Thorp, Margaret, F., 85.12
Thorpe, Earl E., 29.18–19
Thrasher, F. M., 75.1
Thurston, Henry W., 38.13
Tindall, George Brown, 13.17, 29.20
Tilden, Freeman, 14.15
Timberlake, James H., 77.10
Tipple, John O., 67.4
Toole, K. Ross, 16.13
Torbet, Robert G., 63.1
Towley, Louis, 75.11
Tracy, Stanley J., 21.4
Trachtenberg, Alan, 10.14, 81.23
Trattner, Walter I., 38.14–15, 76.12
Trilling, Lionel, 70.15
Trowbridge, John T., 5.6
Tryon, Warren S., 97.8
Tunnard, Christopher, 19.24–25
Turnbull, Andrew, 84.6
Twelve Southerners, 67.5
Twyman, Robert W., 47.11
Tyack, David B., 87.23, 88.1
Tyler, Gus, 75.2
Tyler, Robert L., 52.19

Ulanov, Barry, 81.24
Unger, Irwin, 5.7
U.S. Bureau of the Census, 3.3, 21.5
U.S. Bureau of Education, 92.2
U.S. Bureau of Labor, 50.12
U.S. Department of Agriculture, 41.1
U.S. Department of Interior, 34.10
U.S. Department of Labor, 47.12
U.S. Farm Security Administration, 42.17
U.S. Library of Congress, 3.4
U.S. National Advisory Commission on Civil Disorders, 28.13
U.S. National Museum, 92.3
U.S. National Resources Planning Board, 73.17
U.S. Office of Scientific Research and Development, 98.12
U.S. President's Committee on Migratory Labor, 41.2
U.S. President's National Advisory Commission on Rural Poverty, 72.22
U.S. Public Health Service, 100.20

Vail, Henry Hobart, 84.7
Vance Maurice M., 98.13
Vanderbilt, Kermit, 79.2
Vanorman, Richard A., 14.16
Van Tassel, David D., 98.14
Vaughan, Floyd Lamar, 40.1
Vaughan, Thomas, 17.8
Veblen, Thorstein, 91.7
Vecoli, Rudolph J., 10.15, 25.3
Veiller, Lawrence, 74.6
Vernon, Raymon, 18.9
Vestal, Stanley, 34.11
Veysey, Lawrence R., 91.8
Vidich, Arthur J., 41.13
Viles, Jonas, 91.9
Villard, Oswald Garrison, 95.20
Voigt, David, 86.16

Wade, Louise C., 61.2, 76.13
Wade, Richard C., 19.4
Walker, Mack, 24.12
Walker, Peter F., 5.8
Wallace, David D., 13.18
Wallace, David H., 81.25
Wallace, Irving, 86.17
Wallace, Paul A. W., 10.16
Walls, Otto F., 73.18
Walters, Thorstina, 26.13
Ward, John W., 54.23
Ware, Caroline F., 3.5, 10.17
Ware, Louise, 76.14
Ware, Norman J., 52.20
Warne, Colston E., 52.21
Warner, Hoyt Landon, 72.2
Warner, Sam Bass, Jr., 20.1–3
Warner, William Lloyd, 20.4, 44.20, 53.15, 79.3, 102.13
Warren, Frank A., 69.21
Warren, Harris, 8.25
Warren, Robert Penn, 28.14
Warren, Sidney, 60.3
Washburn, Wilcomb E., 34.12
Washington, Booker T., 33.12
Washington, Joseph R., 32.2

W INDEX

Waskow, Arthur I., 31.2
Wattenberg, Ben J., 21.6
Weatherby, William J., 29.12
Weatherford, W. D., 32.3
Weaver, Richard M., 67.6
Weaver, Warren, 76.15
Webb, Beatrice, 6.6
Webb, Constance, 33.13
Webb, Walter P., 14.17, 15.24, 56.5
Wecter, Dixon, 8.26, 9.11, 21.21, 48.1, 48.6, 84.8
Weinberg, Arthur M., 7.7, 95.21,
Weinberg, Lila, 7.7, 95.21
Weinstein, James, 68.17, 73.19
Weintraub, Hyman, 52.22
Weisberger, Bernard A., 63.2, 96.21-22
Weisenburger, Francis P., 11.15, 60.4-5
Weller, Jack E., 11.17
Welter, Rush, 87.9
Weltfish, Gene. 34.13
Welsch, Erwin K., 28.15
Wentz, Adbel Ross, 63.3
Wesley, Charles H., 32.13
Wesley, Edgar B., 87.10
West, Earl H., 32.4
West, James C. W., 15.25
West, Ray B., 63.4
Weyl, Walter, 67.7
White, C. C., 72.23
White, D. M., 85.8
White, Edward A., 60.6, 98.15
White, Lucia, 20.5
White, Morton G., 20.5, 67.8. 94.9, 94.11
White, William Allen, 95.3
Whitehill, Walter M., 20.6, 92.4-5
Whitener, Daniel Jay, 77.11
Whitlock, Brand, 70.16
Whitnah, Donald R., 101.13
Whitney, David C., 9.17
Whyte, William I., 20.7, 38.16
Widick, B. J., 51.10, 52.23
Wiebe, Robert H., 6.7, 7.8
Wiggins, Sam P., 57.11
Wik, Reynold M., 40.2
Wilbur, Earl Morse, 63.5
Wilcox, Delos F., 96.23
Wilcox, Walter W., 41.3
Wiley, Bell Irvin, 2.19, 5.9, 29.21
Wilkins, Thurman, 82.1, 101.14
Willard, Frances Elizabeth, 36.5-6

Willard, Josiah Flint, 75.3
Williams, Ralph C., 100.21
Williams, Robin M., Jr., 21.22, 102.14
Williamson, Harold F., 46.18
Williamson, Joel, 29.22
Williamson, William L., 92.6
Wilson, Dale, 96.5
Wilson, Edmund, 84.9-13
Wilson, Louis R., 91.10
Wilson, William E., 11 18, 71.5
Wind, Herbert W., 86.18
Winston, Ellen, 9.1
Winters, John D., 5.10
Winther, Oscar O., 14.18, 24.8, 46.19-20
Wirth, Louis, 23.12
Wisbey, Herbert A., Jr., 76.16
Wish, Harvey, 4.3, 32.5, 94.12
Witte, Edwin E., 73.20
Wittke, Carl 11.7, 23.13, 24.9, 24.13-14, 63.6, 82.2, 92.7, 96.24
Wolfe, Tom, 22.1, 38.17, 85.21
Wolfenstein, M., 38.10
Wolff, Leon, 53.16
Wolman, Leo, 53.1-2
Wood, Forrest G., 31.3
Wood, James Playsted, 44.21, 95.22
Wood, Robert C., 20.8
Wood, Stephen B., 38.18
Woodford, Arthur M., 11.19
Woodford, Frank B., 11.19, 100.22
Woodring, Paul, 88.2
Woodroofe, Kathleen, 76.17
Woods, Robert Archey, 72.24-25
Woodward, C. Vann, 5.1, 6.8, 13.19, 31.4, 42.18
Woodward, William E., 4.4
Woody, Thomas, 36.7, 91.11
Woofter, T. J., 9.1
Woolfolk, George R., 54.24
Worthy, Ruth, 33.8
Woytinsky, Emma S., 39.9
Wreston, Michael, 95.23
Wright, Dale, 41.4
Wright, Frank Lloyd, 82.2-3
Wright, Lyle, H., 3.6, 84.14
Wright, Richard, 28.16, 29.23
Wylie, Philip, 37.7
Wyllie, Irvin G., 22.2, 67.9
Wynes, Charles E., 30.1, 31.5
Wytrwal, Joseph A., 25.10

INDEX Y–Z

Yancey, William L., 28.6
Yearley, C. K., 50.13
Yellen, Samuel, 53.17
Yellowitz, Irwin, 39.10, 50.14
Yinger, J. Milton, 34.9
Yorburg, Betty, 68.18
Young, Edwin, 7.20, 48.21
Young, James Harvey, 101.1–2
Young, Kimball, 37.8

Yuan, D. Y., 25.21

Zieger, Robert H., 50.15
Ziff, Larzer, 6.9
Zinn, Howard, 13.20, 31.6, 67.10
Zorbaugh, Harvey, 20.9
Znaniecki, Florian, 25.9
Zornow, William Frank, 15.26, 74.1–2